SEMINAR STUDIES IN HISTORY

Editor: Patrick Richardson

EMPIRE and SLAVERY

SEMINAR STUDIES IN HISTORY

Editor: Patrick Richardson

A full list of titles in this
series will be found on the
back cover of this book

SEMINAR STUDIES IN HISTORY

EMPIRE & SLAVERY

Patrick Richardson

Maps drawn by Leo Vernon

HARPER & ROW, PUBLISHERS
NEW YORK, EVANSTON, SAN FRANCISCO,
LONDON

Library of Congress Catalog Card Number 72–151339

Printed in Malta by St Paul's Press Ltd for Harper & Row, Publishers, Inc.

Contents

Part Three · Conclusion

Part Four · Documents and Tables

Maps

Note on the System of References

A bold number in round brackets (5) in the text refers the reader to the corresponding entry in the Bibliography section at the end of the book.

A bold number in square brackets, preceded by 'doc.' [**docs 6, 8**] refers the reader to the corresponding items in the section of Documents, which follows the main text.

Acknowledgements

We are grateful to Cambridge University Press for permission to include 5 tables from *An Abstract of British Historical Statistics* by Mitchell & Deane.

Introduction

In the eighteenth century England and France established flourishing colonial empires across the Atlantic. The most valuable parts of these empires in the eyes of contemporaries were the plantation colonies of the Caribbean and those in the southern colonies of North America.

Wars were fought in the Caribbean; conquests there were haggled over at the treaties. Both countries built up tightly protectionist economic systems to secure the benefits of the colonies. In mid-century these plantation colonies were cherished by the politically articulate in England and France.

And yet, less than a hundred years later, England had lost her American colonies, France had lost the greatest of her sugar colonies, and the islands of the Caribbean were ruined and abandoned to their fate. A sweeping attack on the foundations of the plantation colonies was launched in England. The slave trade was abolished; slavery itself was abolished; finally, preferential duties were removed, exposing the plantations to the competition of new producers, with which they could not cope.

This transition involved a whole series of major changes. Economic and political thought, strategic thinking, humanitarian attitudes and even cultural values were radically altered. History is about change, and a change of this magnitude needs examining. Historians have studied many aspects of this situation in detail, and have produced many—often conflicting—theories to account for these changes. This book will attempt to examine the plantation system, and to analyse its decline and fall. In doing so, it will be necessary to assess the effect in this area of the major events of the period—the American and French Revolutions, the Industrial Revolution —and the main developments in the realm of ideas—free trade, romanticism, evangelical religion, and the rights of man. Political trends, such as the emergence of the bourgeoisie, will be taken into account as far as they affect the central problem of the collapse of the plantation empires.

In less than a century the plantation colonies declined from being 'the jewel in the diadem' to 'millstones round the neck'. It is important to understand and explain this change in order to understand the period itself.

Part One

THE
PLANTATION
EMPIRES

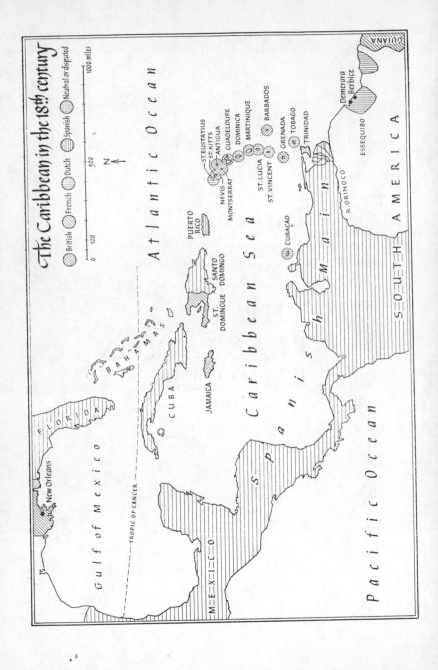

The Caribbean in the 18th century

British ⊘ French ◎ Dutch ◉ Spanish ⊙ Neutral or disputed ⊛

0   100   500   1000 miles

N

Atlantic Ocean

Gulf of Mexico

New Orleans

- - - TROPIC OF CANCER - - -

FLORIDA

B A H A M A S

CUBA

JAMAICA

PUERTO RICO

SANTO DOMINGO

ST. DOMINGUE

ST. EUSTATIUS
ST. KITTS
ANTIGUA
GUADELOUPE
DOMINICA
MARTINIQUE
ST. LUCIA
ST. VINCENT
BARBADOS
GRENADA
TOBAGO
TRINIDAD

NEVIS
MONTSERRAT

CURAÇAO

Caribbean Sea

M—E—X—I—C—O

S p a n i s h   M a i n

R. ORINOCO

Demerara
Berbice

ESSEQUIBO

GUIANA

S O U T H   A M E R I C A

Pacific Ocean

1 The Plantations

In the early seventeenth century Englishmen, Frenchmen and Dutchmen challenged the Spanish and Portuguese monopoly of the New World. All three countries set up colonies in the West Indies and on the eastern seaboard of North America.

The English occupied Barbados in 1625, and St Kitts at about the same time. In 1655 Jamaica was captured from Spain. In addition there were settlements on Nevis, Antigua and Montserrat. In North America the English settled in two main areas. In the south the colony of Virginia was begun on a permanent basis in 1607, and Maryland in 1633. The Carolinas were opened up in 1663, and the final southern colony, Georgia, was founded as a debtors' colony in 1732. Further to the north the English colonised New England, beginning with the Pilgrim Fathers in 1620, and became the only power between Canada and Florida from the final capture of New York from the Dutch in 1674 (**1, 2, 5, 43**).

The French arrived in the West Indies rather later than the English, although they shared St Kitts with them from the beginning until 1702. Their main island colonies were Guadeloupe and Martinique, which were settled in 1635. Grenada and St Lucia became French colonies during the century, while from 1655 the French moved in to the almost deserted northern and western parts of Hispaniola, where they established the great colony of St Domingue, the modern Haiti. In North America the French struggled to occupy the huge wastes of Canada from 1608, and further extended their rather modest man-power by claiming the whole Mississippi Valley down to New Orleans (**4**).

The Dutch had been early in the Caribbean and in North America, but their colonising effort had been too severe for the resources of the young state and by the eighteenth century they had ceased to be a major colonising power in the New World. They were still established in Guiana, and on certain islands in the Caribbean where they set up trading bases. Both the French and the English governments took steps, often disliked or ignored by the colonists, to exclude Dutch traders from their colonies, and in the long run the Dutch commercial dominance was destroyed (**39**).

In spite of this activity, it must not be forgotten that Spain was still far and away the greatest power in the New World, concentrating on the mainland provinces of Mexico and Peru, rather than on the islands. The general decline of Spain, clearly evident by the beginning of the eighteenth century, encouraged other European powers to think in terms of either dismembering the Spanish empire, or of exploiting it by arranging to supply it with slaves and supplies (**40**).

The Portuguese had survived two desperate crises in the sixteenth and seventeenth centuries, when from 1580 to 1640 the country, along with its empire, was annexed by Spain, and from 1624 to 1654 when the Dutch captured and occupied much of Brazil and the complementary slave reservoirs of Portuguese West Africa. In the eighteenth century Portugal had re-established itself as an imperial power with a south Atlantic emphasis.

In the French and English plantation colonies the pattern of development was fairly uniform. At first colonisation was under-capitalised and on a small scale. Most settlers worked small estates, perhaps with a few white servants or bondsmen, growing their own food and producing tobacco as a cash crop. Tobacco could be produced profitably on this scale as long as demand in Europe was not satisfied and prices remained high. These conditions ceased to apply by 1630 and tobacco prices slumped disastrously, due largely to overproduction in Virginia. At this juncture the Dutch introduced sugar from Brazil to the English and French colonies to ensure a large supply for their commercial network and refineries. Very quickly sugar was established as the cash crop for the West Indies. Barbados changed over to sugar production in the 1640s, with Antigua and the French islands following suit rather later. Jamaica began to concentrate on sugar in the second or third decade after its capture, and the huge French colony of St Domingue entered the race in the eighteenth century.

The effect of this change was startling. Sugar cultivation requires capital and fairly large estates. The various stages of production dictate the size of the labour force and capital required. Planting of the canes, manuring and weeding are long and backbreaking jobs in the tropics. The main effort, however, comes at crop time, when the canes have to be cut, and milled very quickly to extract the juice, which then has to be boiled immediately and made into crude sugar and molasses. If there is delay at any of these stages the crop may be ruined or damaged and the returns not worth while (**1, 3**).

In modern conditions a sugar estate can be enormous. Lorry or railway transport, furnace-driven mills using the crushed cane for fuel, and a factory for processing the sugar are available. In the seventeenth and eighteenth centuries these conditions did not apply. The sugar estate had to be around the mill and boiling house, and close enough for the cane to be carried by slaves, or by mules and oxen along inadequate tracks. The mills were slow, and it was touch and go whether the juice could be boiled in time.

The mills, powered by wind or oxen, with their expensive imported rollers, the boiling house with its huge imported coppers, the skilled slave staff in these buildings, the transport animals, the field slave force, and the canes themselves, all involved a considerable outlay of capital, well beyond the early small settlers. But incredibly quickly the size of the estates grew, as the big man squeezed out the small. The price of sugar in Europe remained high, profits were good, slave labour was available, and so the sugar revolution took place.

But sugar cultivation created its own problems. To a lesser extent than tobacco, it exhausts the soil, so that the estate has to be able to take in new land within reach of the mills and boiling house, or the land already used for sugar has to be manured much more heavily—an expensive process—or it has to be planted with new canes much more frequently—again expensive. A cane planted in suitable soil might go on producing, as what was known as a 'ratoon', for five or ten years with a worthwhile return, but in Barbados by the early eighteenth century the soil was so exhausted that an efficient planter would only 'ratoon' for one year at the most (**1, 36**).

But while the returns for sugar were booming, as they were in the seventeenth and early eighteenth centuries, the capital outlay was richly rewarded. As a result, as much land as possible was put down to sugar. Estates cut out the production of whatever else they could. Some food was grown on provision grounds, since this seemed the cheapest way to feed the slave labour force, but everything else was imported from either the mother countries or from North America (**28**).

Barbados was almost completely exploited by 1660, and its sugar production declined throughout the eighteenth century because of soil exhaustion, even though the number of slaves on the island constantly increased. In Jamaica there was much more land available, and new sugar plantations were being cut almost up to the end of the slavery period. Special estates could be organised for crops other than sugar, and for breeding stock. The big planters bought up new plantations or shares in new plantations. In 1737 Peter Beckford, one of the great Jamaican families of sugar 'kings', owned eleven plantations in Jamaica and had shares in five others. As long as there was a frontier with wild country in Jamaica sugar production could go on expanding. But on the whole the British West Indian islands, with the exception of Jamaica, were not big enough for a long period of expansion, and so the men squeezed out by the growth of big estates moved on to new islands or to the later mainland colonies (**29, 35, 36**).

This created a characteristic split in the thinking of West Indian planters. Professor Namier has distinguished between the 'saturated' planters and planters 'on the make' (**51**). Obviously those planters with established estates, probably seeing their returns falling due to soil exhaustion, were not keen to see vast new areas of sugar lands opened up by rival British planters, who would then compete with them for the British market. Thus the planters of Barbados preferred to see French islands remain French, and so excluded from the British market, or, even better, for them to be devastated. The policy of leaving disputed islands such as Dominica, Tobago, St Lucia and St Vincent, unoccupied lasted until 1763, because this suited the influential planter class of the established French and British West Indian islands.

This self-interested attitude developed more clearly in the eighteenth century as financial crisis closed in on the planters. It is seen in the case of Tobago, where Barbadian policy, taken up by the home government, saw Tobago ideally as 'a waste belonging to His Majesty for the use of his subjects' and 'for the use and benefit to Your Majesty's subjects inhabiting Your Majesty's Island of Barbados'. Their fears were to some extent justified, as is shown by the result of the capture and development of the island by the French in 1781, when it instantly became a sugar-producer on a quite formidable scale (**34**).

In the English West Indies the successful planters tended to be absentees. The islands were regarded as a temporary abode, the plantations as a means of piling up enough wealth to enable the owner to return to England, to enter society and perhaps politics in the grand manner. Their property was administered by an attorney, drawing a commission on the produce shipped to England, who was therefore interested in immediate returns, and not in the long-term development of the estate. A white overseer would actually run the estate, with almost unlimited powers. The estate would have to find vast profits to send to the absentee owner for his English establishment, for commissions or salaries for the attorney and overseer, for the upkeep of the 'great house' that was part of every estate, along with its often huge slave household, and for another commission charged by a merchant house in England for handling the produce at that end (**33, 36, 72**).

The French colonists were not absentee on anything like the same scale. As a result their estates did not have to sustain as many charges, and they were able to be administered and developed much more successfully (**29**).

The tobacco colonies of Virginia and Maryland faced slightly different conditions, and as a result developed in their own way. In spite of the catastrophic drop in tobacco prices in the seventeenth century these colonies remained tobacco producers, because they were not climatically suited to sugar, and the potentialities of growing cotton as a staple were not yet apparent either in production techniques or in demand.

Although tobacco exhausts the ground even more rapidly and completely than sugar, this was not an insuperable problem in the vastly bigger mainland colonies. A relatively small proportion of the estate would be under tobacco at any time, and it was simple to move this area around within the estate for some years. If the entire estate was to reach exhaustion point, there were usually lands available to the big buyers in the virgin territories being opened up to the west. The pressure on these lands became very keen, and the governing class, a planter élite of some one hundred families in each colony, used all their backstairs political influence to secure them. While it was not practicable to move a sugar-growing area because of the buildings and machinery involved in the process, this did not apply to the tobacco growers, since the slave gangs, the plants and the drying sheds could be moved easily (**43**).

Furthermore, in Virginia and Maryland there was virtually no absentee problem, except where a big planter owned more than one plantation. Even in that case he would pay frequent visits. In the seventeenth and eighteenth centuries the comparatively wealthy southern colonists sent more children to England for their education than did the northerners, but for the most part they returned to America, where they aimed to live in what they imagined was the style of an English gentleman [**doc. 2**]. For the most part they were hard-working and, to some degree, paternalistic. Their estates were, in the phrase of Professor Boorstin, eighteenth-century versions of the modern company towns (**43**). The peculiar geography of Virginia and Maryland, with its very deeply indented coastline, meant that all the early plantations were easily accessible directly from the sea, and so merchants in England dealt directly with the planters and not through a middleman as they did at first in the sugar colonies. Thus there was little need for harbour towns, and none developed until the later growth of inland plantations made them necessary. The Virginian tidewater plantation provided everything for itself, from doctors to stores and domestic industries. The bigger mainland colonies also tended to be far more self-supporting for food, horses and timber than the islands, and this made trade a less complex problem.

So the English and French colonies in the West Indies and on the mainland of the southern half of North America developed economically in much the same way. Large, heavily capitalised estates had become the norm. All of them relied entirely on the labour of unskilled, expendable, and easily disciplined negro slaves. They were as much a part of the plantation empires of the eighteenth century as the planters or the crops. Their rôle must now be examined.

2 The Slaves

Once it was apparent that huge profits could be made from the cultivation of sugar in the West Indies, and to a lesser extent from tobacco in the southern colonies of North America, it became obvious that negro slavery was the only practicable type of labour. In 1672, when the Royal African Company was formed to ship slaves from Africa to the British plantations, it was stated they 'could not subsist without them' (**19**). John Pinney, the Bristol merchant who made his fortune as a plantation owner, wrote: 'Negroes are the sinews of a Plantation, and it is impossible for a Man to make sugar without the assistance of the Negroes, as to make Bricks without Straw' (**30**).

In the description of the plantation economy in the previous chapter it was shown that sugar and tobacco were labour-intensive crops. For both large, unskilled work-gangs were necessary. Slavery was clearly the most effective method of keeping such large numbers of men working very hard on relatively small areas of land, which, in some colonies, were surrounded by waste land from which they could have scratched some sort of living [**doc. 3**]. It was generally agreed in the eighteenth century that even liberal wages would not have secured the sort of labour needed for plantations, and we shall see that this was a major worry at the time of the emancipation of the slaves in 1833, so that a condition of semi-slavery, known as apprenticeship, was then planned for a further ten years.

The size of a plantation labour force was fixed by the maximum demands of crop time, and this meant that the slaves could have been underemployed for the parts of the year when they were not planting or cutting cane. The planters got round this difficulty by continuing to use such antiquated agricultural methods as hoeing rather than ploughing throughout the eighteenth century, since this could be done by an unskilled labour force and needed no further capital expenditure on machinery or animals. But it must be stressed that this profligate use of labour, which demanded 300 slaves for a 300-acre estate, was for mass production of cash crops, and was planned to make the maximum profits (**1, 3**) [**doc. 2**].

Slavery was the economic solution of this particular labour problem. Europeans could, and still can, work successfully in these climatic conditions, but because a slave was bought for life it was calculated that one Negro slave was worth four or five white indented servants, who were only bound for a five or ten year period and expected slightly higher standards of upkeep (**3**). But the real cost of a slave labour force was never calculated in the eighteenth century, and it is almost impossible to do so now. Professor Pares estimated that about 35 per cent of a planter's capital was tied up in slaves and land planted with canes, and that the haphazard and unbudgeted way of restocking with slaves at intervals was the chief cause of his running up debts (**29**).

The slave system was a snare and delusion to the planters. They assumed that slaves, once bought, involved no further outlay, and therefore could be used wastefully. Although planters almost invariably economised on food and clothing for the slaves, these remained a considerable item, and the planter was also responsible for the upkeep of aged slaves, female slaves about to have or just having had babies, and young boys and girls before they could be put profitably to work. A breakdown of a slave force of 150 shows there were an on average, thirty old people and twenty-five infants [**docs 5, 6**]. Adam Smith wrote with a good degree of truth: 'Work done by slaves, though it appears to cost only their maintenance, is in the end the dearest of any.'

Harsh discipline, amounting all too often to cruelty, seems to have been a concomitant of the slave system. To get regular and long hours of backbreaking work from the slaves, corporal punishment was inevitable. When these powers were wielded as they were by a low-class, partially uneducated white overseer, whose only interest was in high production, and their execution was in the hands of promoted slaves, known as drivers, abuses were almost inevitable. Furthermore, a slave had no remedy at law. The plantation colonies continually passed laws allowing slaves to be punished viciously, and the planter class saw to it that any legislation enforced upon it by the home government favouring the slaves was either insignificant or could be safely ignored. A Carolina planter in 1802 wrote: 'It is a pity that agreeable to the nature of things Slavery and Tyranny must go together and that there is no such thing as having an obedient and useful Slave, without the painful exercise of undue and tyrannical authority' (**48**). Clearly the treatment of the slaves would be liable to deteriorate in the absence of the owner, and this sanction would become increasingly necessary to the planters when the population ratio between Europeans and slaves tilted more and more heavily towards the slaves, as it did wherever the plantation system became established.

A plantation colony involved the reduction of the white population, as the study of any such colony's population figures shows this (**1**). In Barbados, the first island to turn to sugar, there were less than a thousand slaves in 1640, immediately before sugar was introduced by the Dutch. Within five years there were 5,000 slaves to a population of some 40,000 Europeans. Forty years later there were 46,000 slaves on the island while the European population had declined by half. By the turn of the century the slave population had settled down to this figure of 46,000, while the Europeans had been reduced to only 12,000. In 1833 at emancipation, there were 66,000 slaves on the island (**35**).

The other sugar colonies, both British and French, followed suit. Jamaica had 9,500 slaves to 7,700 Europeans in 1673: fifty years later there were 74,000 slaves, while the white population had not grown at all. By 1834 there were 311,070 slaves in Jamaica and not more than 30,000 whites (**33**). The plantation colonies in America became slave-based in the eighteenth century. In 1714 there were only 59,000 slaves in the colonies, but by mid-century the figure had increased to nearly 300,000, and Georgia, which had been founded as a non-slave colony, turned over to slavery in 1750. By the end of the century, when the cotton gin had made plantation cultivation of cotton possible, the slave population of the southern states was approaching 700,000.

Obviously in these conditions of a huge and bitterly resentful captive labour force and a small ruling group, outbreaks of slave violence were inevitable. The earliest slave rising in Barbados was in 1649, and they continued in all islands up to emancipation, rising to a dreadful crescendo in the St Domingue revolution at the beginning of the nineteenth century. The only alternatives to revolt for a slave were escape or suicide. In a small island colony like Barbados the former was virtually impossible; in a big island like Jamaica it was much more common, as was shown by the famous Maroons, runaway slaves living in the hills, who were able to fight

11

campaigns against regular troops, until a treaty with the Maroons included a clause by which they were paid a bounty for capturing runaways (**33**).

Where planters or their representatives regarded slaves as replaceable tools for producing sugar—and this was a common attitude, well shown by such remarks as 'the Negroes come here ready made, the bags of sugar have yet to be made'—the system depended on constant fresh supplies of slaves reaching the plantation colonies from Africa. None of the West Indian plantation colonies maintained their slave population in the eighteenth century. For example Barbados imported 200,000 slaves between 1712 and 1768, at an annual average of 3,570, but in those years the slave population only increased by a total of 26,000, or an annual average of 465.

Certainly the wastage figure was highest in the British sugar colonies with their normally absentee proprietors, but it was also noticeable that the slave population of French islands fell sharply whenever war conditions prevented slave traders reaching those islands. This wastage was over and above the high death rate of slaves on the passage from Africa to the colonies. It has been estimated that up to a third of the slaves arriving in the colonies died during the first three years. This may have been due to their poor condition on arrival, to their inability to cope with diseases that were new to them, or even to a total despair at their loss of freedom and the harsh circumstances of their new lives.

Planters made their own arrangements to feed their slaves, and the fundamental principle appears to have been to avoid this being a charge on the estate, as far as possible. Some estates gave their slaves rum, which had been made on the plantation, and which could be exchanged for food by the slave; others allowed the slaves Saturdays and Sundays to work on the provision grounds to grow their own food. Where necessary, planters provided cheap salt cod from Newfoundland, but very rarely meat, except for some favoured household slaves, and as a result slaves from parts of Africa where it was customary to eat meat were more difficult to sell in the colonies. It is significant that the French *Code Noir*, which was considered too liberal in the colonies, only specified a daily protein ration for a slave equivalent to one kipper. Naturally on such a diet a slave built up very little resistance to disease, and this may partly account for the extraordinarily high infant mortality (**29**).

Another factor accounting for the failure of the slave population to maintain itself was that plantations tended to discourage slaves from breeding, since it was held that it was cheaper to buy a slave than to breed one, and that marriage bonds might prove distracting to the slave and make it more difficult to sell the man or woman separately. In any event, plantations tended to concentrate on one sex of slaves, usually males. Some planters, among them John Pinney, believed female slaves to be more reliable and considerably more docile, and he gave instructions that his plantations were to use females wherever possible (**30**).

To the lack of anything approaching family life on many plantations was added a cultural vacuum. African songs and dances were usually discouraged in the plantations, as tending to remind the slaves of their previous environment, and possibly keeping fresh their tribal loyalties, so tending to make them more difficult. Finally the slaves were discouraged from practising their old religions, again not completely successfully, but at the same time they were firmly prevented on most plantations from attending Christian services, as these were held to be inflammatory and opposed to the concept of slavery (**33, 36, 37**).

So the explosive tensions of slavery were knit into the political, social and economic structure of the plantation colonies. While some colonies, as we shall see, eventually realised that it was in their interests to abolish the slave trade, to maintain their position against newer and underslaved colonies, no plantation colony ever accepted the idea that a plantation could survive without slavery itself. But as it required an ever bigger labour force to produce the same or a smaller amount of sugar from the exhausted soil, so the dependence of the plantation system on the slave trade remained complete. We should now see how this trade fitted into the general picture of the plantation economies.

3 The Slave Trade

Since the plantation colonies did not consider the possibility of any alternative labour system to slavery, and since they were mostly incapable of maintaining, let alone expanding, their slave population, the whole system depended on the continuing importation of slaves—on the African slave trade. It is generally acknowledged that the plantation colonies, especially those in America, could not have pushed back the wilderness to carve out plantations as they did without an almost unlimited supply of slaves transported across the Atlantic by European and American slavers.

When it is realised that more than two million African slaves were transported to British colonies alone between 1680 and 1783, it will be seen what powerful interests were involved. Some idea of the concern about the trade can be got from reading the lists of petitions to Parliament after 1688, when it was hoped that the monopolistic Royal African Company might be abolished and the trade opened to all comers. K. G. Davies has described the great political battle on this issue, and he shows that the idea of free trade in slaves was supported by all sorts of manufacturing interests in England, by the shipowners and merchants of outports such as Bristol and Liverpool, and by plantation owners in the colonies, who, in some cases mistakenly, hoped for a greatly increased supply of slaves (**19**).

Since the highly prized plantation empires so clearly relied on the slave trade, and because there were so many powerful voices in support of it [**docs 11, 12**], the governments of France and England made it a cardinal object of policy to gain as big a share of the trade as possible, to guarantee their nationals' position on the coast of Africa, and to ensure that their colonies were supplied by their own merchants and ships.

England and France both set up slaving castles on the coast of Africa, the English based on Cape Coast Castle, and the French in Gorée and Senegal. From these bases and their tributary posts—they

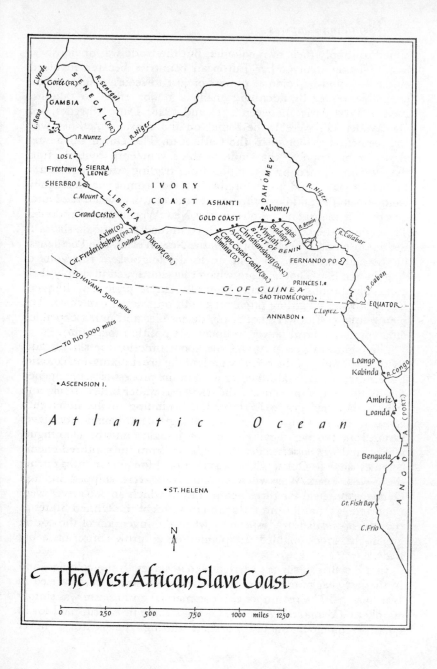

The West African Slave Coast

aimed to supply their own colonies. But the trade was obviously so lucrative that many other European countries became involved, either as would-be colonial powers or just to secure a share of the profitable trade. Brandenburg made a major effort to establish itself in West Africa between 1711 and 1748; Danes, Swedes, and Courlanders all were to be found on the coast, sometimes with complementary colonies in the Caribbean. The Dutch threatened almost to monopolise the trade in the seventeenth century, until they were excluded by legislation from trading with English and French colonies and were forcibly ejected from their Portuguese conquests in the middle of the seventeenth century, when the Dutch dream of a plantation empire in the New World was abandoned. Throughout the century the Dutch continued to smuggle slaves to the Spanish and French colonies in the New World. The Portuguese in the end were able to hold on to the huge slave reservoirs of Angola and São Thomé, from which they continued to supply their great plantations in Brazil. Naturally, in a period of frequent European wars, fighting often broke out on the African coast. The picturesque castles were not really defensible, and much depended on a country's naval power to uphold its position there (**20**).

The eighteenth century was the boom time for the slave trade. By the beginning of the century most of the great plantation colonies were either firmly established or were in the process of being opened up. By the end of the century the trade was under bitter attack, and it was abolished gradually from the beginning of the nineteenth century. In the eighteenth century the greatest demand for slaves came from the big sugar colonies of Jamaica and St Domingue, where land was easier to get than labour; from the captured enemy colonies, such as Cuba, which was occupied for nine months during the Seven Years War when 10,000 slaves were shipped in, and Guadeloupe, held for three years, during which 40,000 slaves were imported (**31**); and from the southern states of the United States at the end of the century, especially when the invention of the cotton gin in the 1790s enabled the plantations to grow cotton on a big scale.

In 1760 British slavers carried 38,000 slaves to the colonies, and in the last year of the trade in 1806–7 49,000 slaves were carried in British ships. The reason for this commercial enthusiasm was simply supply and demand. While the cost of a slave in Africa, paid for in goods, remained roughly constant during the century, never exceeding £25, the selling price in the colonies rose fairly steadily In 1700, the end of the monopoly period, prices were about £20 against a purchase price of £12; by 1728 the selling price had risen to £30. In the 1740s slaves were fetching £37 in the colonies, and during the wars of the American and French Revolutions the price rose as high as £50 to £80. Costs were rising throughout the period, and during a war there was a very real risk of attack by enemy cruisers or privateers, but nevertheless a successful slave voyage remained a profitable concern. For example, the slaver *Enterprise*, out of Liverpool in 1803, carried 326 slaves to Jamaica, where they averaged over £60 per head, and 412 slaves to Havana. The cost to the owners of equipping the ship was just over £8,000, and the cost of goods to exchange for slaves was £8,900. The profit for the voyage was £24,430 (**18, 22**) [**doc. 8**].

But the success of the slave trade depended on complete flexibility of operation. During the commercial life of the Royal African Company in the seventeenth century, the lesson had been learnt that a slaving policy based on fair shares for all colonies with generous credit for the planters had only one result—bankruptcy for the supplier. When the trade was thrown open, the total number of slaves increased enormously and at once, but the small private traders who now appeared on the scene legally had only one interest, and that was maximum profit. Thus if prices were higher in expanding Jamaica than in saturated Barbados, then the slavers sailed to Jamaica or forced Barbadians to pay those prices. If a colony tried to pay with its own currency or in kind at rates fixed locally in the planters' favour, the slavers quickly lost interest and refused to deliver to that colony. Again, if there was trouble on the coast of Africa or if there was a possibility of war, the private trader tended not to risk his ship. In the conditions of free trade, slaving was left to the traders to make what profit they could, and it was not seen solely as a necessary adjunct of the plantation system. Thus it became of enormous interest to private traders to supply goods and slaves to the Spanish islands, since prices there were high and the slaves were paid for in silver coins. But British planters regarded any such trade with horror, partly because they felt that an alternative market for slaves in the New World would push up prices, and partly because they saw slaves being sent to foreign colonies that might come to compete with them for the European market (**19**).

This resulted in the vexed problem of the *Asiento*, the licence to supply Spanish colonies with a stated number of slaves per annum. This prospect was regarded with great favour by the home government and by important commercial interests in the City of London, where the notorious South Sea Company was created in theory to trade with the *Asiento* negotiated in the Treaty of Utrecht in 1714. The failing Royal African Company made its last great effort to supply the new company with its quota of slaves for the Spanish islands. In fact the *Asiento* was never a profitable licence, and much money was lost in its operation. It had the undoubted effect of exciting European interest in the slave trade, in African trading posts and in the Caribbean colonies (**54**).

Apart from the colonial interest in the delivery of slaves, there were many other points at which the slave trade created concern in England. The amount of shipping and the number of sailors engaged on the slaving voyages were often quoted as reasons for the trade continuing. Professor MacInnes, however, examined the register of Bristol slave ships in the eighteenth century, and he found that the ships were usually old and small, the majority being from 75 to 150 tons burden. They would probably not have been of much use to the fleet or to the merchant marine in any other capacity (**27**).

The question of seamen involved is more problematical. For many years the Royal Navy regarded the slave trade as a nursery for seamen second only to the fisheries. It was true that a slaver carried a larger crew per hundred tons than a West Indiaman, at the ratio of about 12:7, but of these many were not able-bodied seamen, having been shipped only to supervise the slave cargo. The main reason for the heavier crewing ratio was the mortality among crews on the voyages. Figures are not very reliable about the death rate, many of them being provided by abolitionists, but it appears that among the crews on the slaving voyages it was about 20 per cent, which is about the same as the slave death rate on the voyages. The sea shanty chorus

> Beware and take care the Bight of Benin,
> There's one comes out for forty goes in.

is a characteristic seaman's exaggeration of a grim truth.

The structure of the slave trade was triangular. This involved three stages of the voyage, each of which, in theory, could show a profit for the backers. A cargo of trading goods was loaded at one

of the European ports connected with the slave trade, London
Bristol or Liverpool in England, and Nantes in France, or from one
of the American slaving ports, for the most part in New England,
such as Newport in Rhode Island. The trading goods used to buy
African slaves became more and more specialised: textiles from
England and from the East; hats and caps; all sorts of hardware,
such as swords, daggers and knives; guns; trash such as beads and
bells; and certain basic commodities that were almost currency on
the coast, notably iron bars and salt. From America very cheap
tobacco was sent, and more and more rum, distilled in New
England. An American captain in 1736 showed that the Americans
were liable to flood the market, almost literally, with this spirit. He
wrote from the coast: 'Heair is 7 sail of us Rume men that
we are Ready to Devur one another; for our Case is despart'
(**38**).

These cargoes were then taken to the slaving stations on the west
coast of Africa where it was hoped they would be exchanged as
quickly as possible for cargoes of healthy slaves of working age.
Sometimes there would be slaves waiting in the dungeons and
barracoons of the castles; sometime a slave merchant would have
an agent on the coast who would have collected a cargo in readiness.
On occasions captains would have to get slaves by any method they
could. The great essential was speed, since slaves and crews were
prone to contract fevers (**22**).

The slaves were then carried across the Atlantic to the plantation
colonies, where they were sold either directly to planters, who had
to be given due warning by colony law, to agents, who might prepare
the slaves for a better sale at a later date, or to a local merchant,
who would act as a middle man. The slaver would take payment in
cash if there was any available in the colony, in bills of exchange
redeemable in London, or in kind, carrying away sugar, tobacco
or other colonial produce. The Americans concentrated increasingly
on returning with a cargo of molasses, the raw material for their
thriving distilleries.

Theoretically at least, there was a profit to be made on each leg
of the triangle, but in fact there were also problems at each stage.
On the coast there might not be a cargo of slaves ready, and delay
was dangerous and expensive. The goods taken out might not be
in demand at that exact time. On the voyage across the Atlantic—
the notorious Middle Passage—up to a third of the slaves might die

in normal conditions, while there was also a real risk of disease, mutiny [**doc. 9**] or, in the event of war, of capture.

In the colonies the slaver was to some extent exploited by colonial law. He had to give up-country planters time to attend the sale; he might have to accept payment in kind at rates fixed heavily in the planters' favour; there might be a fixed price in effect in the colony; there might even be some unacceptable local currency substitute offered, or there might be a heavy import duty to be paid. Of course the slaver had the ultimate answer. He could always sail on to a better market in another colony, but this caused delay and probably more deaths among his cargo and desertions among his crew (**29**).

The greatest problem faced by the slaver in the colonies was payment. The planter assumed that a slaver would give him long term credit. To some extent this was necessary, as there was a long time between crops, but the planters seemed to have demanded quite unrealistically long periods in which to pay. The Royal African Company used up its whole capital in carrying this massive debt for unpaid for slaves, and the private trader was only a little better off (**19**).

Finally, the last leg was fraught with difficulties. The cargo collected in the colonies might be of poor quality, or there might be a glut on the home market on arrival. Occasionally huge profits were made on the triangular voyages, but there were also many risks, and during the century the tendency was for the trade to be taken over by larger companies with several ships, who could afford to pay agents where it suited the trade, and who were not put out of business by one set of disappointing returns. In the control of these merchants, the slave trade remained articulate to the end, but the fact that fewer people were involved meant that it could be attacked more easily.

While several industries found valuable markets directly from the slave trade, the greatest effect was on the growth of ports in England, France and America. In the seventeenth century, when the slave trade had been conducted solely by the Royal African Company, London to all intents and purposes had an English monopoly. This provoked the noisy disgust of certain outports, notably Bristol. When the trade was opened at the turn of the century to all merchants ready to pay a 10 per cent charge, Bristol immediately challenged London for control of the trade. By 1725 the west country port was sending ships to carry almost as many slaves to the colonies as was London, with 17,000 slaves in Bristol ships to 26,000 in those from the capital. By mid-century Liverpool had emerged as the leading slave port in the country. Bristol had been an important port for centuries, and it had only received a boost from the slave trade; Liverpool evolved from a mere village to a great port on the strength of the trade alone. It had the advantage of the growing industrial hinterland of Lancashire, but its success seems to have stemmed from a slaving fever in the town. This is well expressed in a book in 1795: 'Almost every man in Liverpool is a merchant, and he who cannot send a bale will send a band-box ... almost every order of people is interested in a Guinea cargo, it is to this influenza that there are so many small ships.'

In addition the Liverpool shipowners seem to have paid their seamen less than London or Bristol, to have economised on the crew's food and the captain's perquisites, and to have driven much harder bargains. In any case, Liverpool became the British slaving port *par excellence*. By the end of the century a third of all its shipping was in the trade, and Liverpool ships were responsible for $\frac{5}{8}$ of the whole British trade. Estimates of the profits vary, but a reasonable contemporary calculation put those of the Liverpool trade between 1783 and 1793 at 30 per cent. With Liverpool's dramatic rise to prominence, Bristol and London became more interested in other trades, while Glasgow was only secondarily a slave port. In Liverpool, as in London and Bristol, the trade tended to fall into the control of about ten big firms, and by the end of the century there are definite signs that these were beginning to feel the pinch (**3, 18, 49**).

While the slave trade was vital to the plantations and to the whole elaborate economic system of which they were the base, it can be seen that the trade was also of importance to various industries in Britain, to importers from the East, to merchants in America and Britain, and to the very existence of Liverpool and the growth of Bristol in the eighteenth century. The trade, like the plantations, was a strong vested interest, but its aims did not always coincide with those of the planters.

4 Protection

These European colonial empires in the western hemisphere were valuable, and the parent states were determined that this wealth should come back to them. As a result these countries passed legislation to exclude foreign merchants, foreign goods and foreign ships from the trade of their own colonies. These systems of protection were attacked by economists towards the end of the eighteenth century, when they were stigmatised as 'mercantilism', but this is such a loose and emotive term that it has ceased to serve much purpose. 'Mercantilism', if it means anything, is a policy instituted to benefit the merchants or the commerce of a country, and as a result it can be applied equally to the Dutch policies of free trade in certain parts of the world in this period, or to the rigidly exclusive policies of the other countries (**39, 66**).

In the eyes of protectionists the colonies existed to supply the mother countries with any commodities they produced that were not produced in the mother country. These were either for home consumption or for re-exporting. In the former case there would be less need to import from foreigners, and in the latter the favourable balance of trade would bring into the country the hard cash that was seen as real wealth by economists and politicians at that time.

However, the system also benefited the colonies to some extent. The colonists had the advantage of a preferential market in the mother country; they were often paid subsidies for producing commodities particularly needed at home; they were protected against enemies during wars and against privateers and pirates in peacetime; efforts were made to provide immigrants and slaves for the colonies; technical advice and capital were often provided. The French called the arrangement for their colonies the *Pacte colonial* which implies the idea of it being mutually advantageous (**40**).

But these compensations were not enough to stop the system of protection being a burden to the colonies. By canalising colonial trade to the mother country, the margin of profit for the colonists was obviously cut. They would have preferred to sell in the widest possible market, since under protection any colonial goods re-exported from the mother country did not profit them but a middleman in the parent country. In addition they had no choice but to use the mother country's or colonial shipping, and this might well involve them in unnecessarily high freight rates. There would be unavoidable duties to pay in the home country.

An estimate has put the cost of the monopoly system and the duties to the colonies in America alone in the 1770s at between £500,000 and £1,500,000 p.a. But against this must be set the cost of colonial wars, defence forces and administration borne by the mother country. Both England and France paid out more money than they received from levies on trade. In 1789 France spent £668,000, while only receiving £275,000 in direct revenue. It must be concluded that neither England nor France regarded their colonies as revenue-producing, but that their value overall, both commercial and strategic, made their cost worth while (**44, 45**).

This outline may suggest that the idea of protection was the result of systematic thinking to meet the colonial situation. This was not the case. From a piecemeal start the machinery of protection accumulated until a comprehensive system had been established to control the wealth of the colonies. Then, as the colonies became more and more valuable, the system of protection connected with the colonies was regarded as fundamental to colonial success, and therefore became sacrosanct.

When Spain and Portugal established overseas empires in the fifteenth and sixteenth centuries it was considered natural and inevitable that they should set up very exclusive systems of protection. These were, and remained, rigid, involving single ports in the home countries for all colonial trade, monopoly groups of merchants, annual fleets to and from the colonies, and an absolute veto, in practice not always observed, on all traffic with foreigners (**40**).

While Spain and Portugal had the shipping, industry and agriculture to service their colonies, and the naval power to protect them, other countries interloped at risk. But since neither Spain nor Portugal was able to maintain these commercial monopolies into the seventeenth century, the Dutch and the English quickly broke into their empires. The Dutch became the great suppliers and shippers of goods to and from the Caribbean and Brazil. When the English and French set up island colonies in the western hemisphere in the early seventeenth century, it was largely as a result of Dutch support and encouragement in terms of credit and services, and under cover of Dutch naval power.

By the middle of the century the Dutch were so dominant in European commerce that the French and the English took identical and almost simultaneous measures against them. It was these measures that formed the protection systems of the two rival empires in the eighteenth century, and it is not an exaggeration to say that the colonial commercial policy of the two great imperial powers of the eighteenth century was determined by envy of the Dutch.

The strongly mercantile Rump Parliament of the English republic passed an Ordinance in 1651 that outlined all later protectionist policy. This stated that goods grown or manufactured in Asia, Africa or America were only to come to England in ships owned and commanded by Englishmen, and crewed by a majority of English sailors. Goods of foreign origin were to come direct to England, and not through the hands of middlemen. Goods grown in Europe were only to go to England or English possessions in ships belonging to England or to the country where the goods originated. This legislation was not predominantly colonially centred, but it was all aimed, and aimed successfully, at the Dutch commercial network, which was not based on Dutch production to any great extent.

There were inefficiencies in this first attempt, and the Navigation Act of 1660 set out to close the loopholes. This stated that all goods of whatever origin were to go in and out of the colonies in English or English colonial ships. Three-quarters of the crews, the master and the owner of the ships had to be English or English colonials. Certain colonial goods particularly needed in England, known as 'enumerated' goods, including sugar, cotton, ginger, indigo, dyewoods and tobacco, could only be marketed in Britain. It should be noticed that this Act did not cut out the already thriving American colonial shipping industry, which indeed was always encouraged by the British government as being conducive to total British maritime strength. The clause about enumerated goods put the valuable re-export trade, applicable notably to Virginian tobacco, into English, and later Scottish, hands.

Subsequent Acts added refinements to the system. The 1663 Staple Act required all European produced goods, with the exception of salt, servants and wine, to pass through England, again giving English merchants an unassailable position as middlemen, but also adding considerably to the price of goods in the colonies. The 1673 Navigation Act put teeth into the system by making a ship leaving a colony with 'enumerated' goods pay a bond equal to the duties to be paid on the goods on arrival in England. The aim here was to make the smuggling of goods to non-British ports unprofitable. The 1696 Navigation Act set up special Vice-Admiralty courts in the colonies to deal with offences arising under the Navigation Acts.

This was the system of protection that remained unchanged in principle throughout the eighteenth century, and was not finally done away with until 1849. From 1707, following the Act of Union, Scots were considered as the equals of the English, and quickly became the most important factors of Virginian tobacco. A major concession to the West Indian colonies was made in 1739, when they were allowed to ship sugar direct to Europe, south of Cape Finisterre.

The pattern and timing of French protection were more or less identical with the English. From 1661 Colbert directed French economic policy against the Dutch in every way at his disposal, and this of course involved the colonies. Since French colonial policy was concerned as much with increasing national power as with creating private wealth, the state backed chartered monopoly company was the first method used. But, as the Dutch and the French both found, it was too much for a company to subsidise a young colony and also to pay dividends, and Colbert's companies collapsed in the seventeenth century.

The final form of French mercantilism appeared with the *Pacte colonial* of 1698. This summarised a series of proclamations excluding foreigners from French colonial trade in both directions, and ensuring this commerce passed exclusively through French ports, thus giving a tremendous boost to French west coast ports, in particular Nantes and La Rochelle. The French system was less exclusive than the Spanish, since French colonial trade was open to all French subjects sailing from any French port, but it was more restrictive than the British system, since all French colonial produce had to be shipped to France. In addition the government legislated in favour of French brandy distillers by banning the import of rum or molasses from the French islands. During the eighteenth century home brandy refineries were favoured at the expense of the colonies.

During the eighteenth century French protection became very burdensome to the colonists, French shipping was constantly harassed in wartime; supplies, which had to come right across the Atlantic, became scarcer and so more expensive; freight charges rose steadily. The rapidly increasing sugar output of the French islands and the all-important part played by colonial trade in the French economy, where it accounted for more than two-fifths of all French exports, did little to recompense French planters, and since patriotism was never a striking characteristic of any West Indian colonists, it is not surprising to find French islands negotiating to become British during the slave revolts connected with the French Revolution (34).

Although direct Dutch influence in the Caribbean was eventually destroyed by the protection systems of France and England, the Dutch managed to maintain commercial importance in the Caribbean area by introducing the idea of 'free ports'. Their little island of St Eustatius became the most prosperous port in the Caribbean, acting as an entrepôt for the Spanish and French islands in particular. Both England and France were jealous of this success, and there was strong pressure from the West Indian interest in England to establish free ports in Jamaica and other islands. This was finally done in 1766. The French were not prepared to let the English steal a march on them, and they opened free ports of their own from 1767. As the Spanish had finally decided to abandon the idea of licensing monopoly companies to import their slaves and were ready to throw the trade open to all comers, there was clearly enormous and profitable business to be done. The free port idea did not destroy protectionism, but surrendered a non-essential aspect to keep the fundamental idea intact. The French had a nice phrase for the new state of affairs—*l'exclusif mitigé* (4, 32).

A fundamental aspect of protection was the belief held by contemporaries that it was created to sustain naval power. It will be seen that this was the overriding motive behind much political action connected with the colonies. The system of protection reveals the true relationship between the parent countries and their colonies. Edmund Burke called this link 'purely commercial'. In 1765 the French Minister of Marine wrote to the governor of Martinique: 'The colonies are absolutely nothing but commercial establishments.' This attitude is basic to the whole problem of empire in the eighteenth century [**doc. 26**]. As long as the colonies were commercially successful, prices pushed up by the production monopoly and cruelties as apparent as those connected with the slave trade and slavery itself could be accepted. But if the colonies should fail to fill their economic rôle, there would be little sentiment to prevent them being swept aside in favour of more promising commercial prospects.

Finally it must be stressed that the colonies did not object specifically to the system of protection. Some of them as high cost producers grew to rely on the closed markets of the mother country; the West Indian colonies in particular depended absolutely upon the naval power of the mother country for protection. When the First Continental Congress of the American colonies issued the American Declaration of Rights in 1774, it was clearly stated:

We cheerfully consent to the operation of such Acts of the British Parliament, as are *bona fide*, restrained to the regulation of our external commerce, for the purpose of securing the commercial advantages of the whole empire to the mother country, and the commercial benefits of its respective members.

This attitude of the Americans may seem surprising, but it supports the belief of the home governments of the time that central control of colonial trade was necessary and was imposed primarily to subordinate the selfish aims of various interested parties. This ideal could never be achieved to the satisfaction of all, but the lasting nature of the system suggests that it was at least partially implemented.

5 The American Interest

All the British colonies in North America and the French colonies in Canada and Louisiana were included in the systems of protection. Both groups of colonies played an important part in the imperial schemes of their mother countries, but they also presented problems and created strains within the systems.

Plantation colonies tended towards specialisation and even monoculture, and as a result they became virtually dependent on imported food and supplies. In theory these were to be provided by the mother country, with the colonies providing a closed market for home agriculture and industry. In the eighteenth century the practice was not quite so simple.

In the early eighteenth century the non-plantation colonies further to the north were regarded with some suspicion by economists, since they appeared not to be capable of contributing to the imperial economy. They produced no valuable staple crops, since their agriculture was similar to that of Europe; there were few industries, since these were banned by the metropolitan governments if they seemed likely to rival home manufactures; and as markets they were inconsiderable, because they had a relatively small and poor population. In every way they were less attractive than the plantation colonies.

But during the eighteenth century this situation changed. The northern colonies grew both in population and in wealth. In 1715 the population of the colonies was estimated at 434,600: sixty years later it was 2,554,500, with more than 400,000 slaves. By 1760 £1,760,000 of exports from Britain were coming into the American colonies. New England and New York both took more than £300,000 worth per annum, and Pennsylvania was not far behind. Virginia and Maryland combined were the only bigger importers. This growing demand presented a problem for the American colonists, since only the southern plantation colonies were exporting enough to the mother country to pay for these imports.

How could the difference be made good? (**44, 45, 46**) [**doc. 4**].

The British colonists in North America solved this problem to some extent by making themselves the agricultural complement of the plantation colonies. They provided practically all the non-industrial supplies needed by the plantations, and, because they were nearer the plantations and possessed highly competitive shipping services, they were able to undersell rivals from the British Isles. The middle colonies, in particular Pennsylvania and Virginia, provided oats, corn, flour, peas and beans for all the plantation colonies. Philadelphia and Baltimore grew into major ports on this trade. From New England came livestock—horses, sheep, hogs and poultry—timber for housing and for the barrels for sugar and molasses, and fish, either caught by New Englanders or shipped through them from the Newfoundland fisheries. Even a few manufactured goods, such as soap and candles, managed to avoid British disapproval and were shipped to the plantations (**28**) (E.H.D. ix).

The plantation colonies varied in their dependence on the American trade. Barbados, completely turned over to sugar before 1700, needed everything; Jamaica still had land not under sugar all through the eighteenth century, but nevertheless became increasingly tied to the American colonies; Virginia and Maryland, with their own hinterlands for timber, imported some foodstuffs from Pennsylvania and New England.

But this was not the whole story. The northern colonists were extremely enterprising traders and soon built an elaborate economic superstructure on this fairly simple trade. In return for the agricultural goods they sent to the plantations, the Americans took unrefined sugar or molasses, the raw material for rum, in payment. Since there was always a shortage of currency in eighteenth-century colonies, this exchange suited the planters. The unrefined sugar and the molasses were shipped back to the northern colonies, where a network of refineries and distilleries was established.

The resulting sugar and rum were at first consumed in the colonies, in the fisheries, and in the logging camps. As long as the price of molasses and unrefined sugar remained low in the British colonies there was a very worthwhile margin of profit. This was increased when American merchants realised that they too could open up a triangular trade, carrying rum to Africa to buy slaves, who were then carried to the Caribbean or the southern colonies to be exchanged for more of the raw materials needed from the plantations.

At first this commercial system could be contained within the British empire, but as the Americans extended their enterprises they demanded more and more unrefined sugar and molasses. The British sugar colonies, from which most sugar was shipped to England and where much of the molasses was distilled locally, could not produce enough and their prices began to creep up. The American merchants soon discovered a better source of supply in the French plantation colonies in the Caribbean.

There were several reasons why the French colonies answered American requirements so well. French production of sugar was increasing rapidly during the century, and there was no alternative market for their molasses, since the French government had forbidden the manufacture of rum in the French colonies in order to protect the home brandy industry. In addition, supplies to the French colonies were erratic and expensive, since French shipping was frequently stopped by wars. The French colonies did not receive the necessary supplies from Canada, which produced timber and fish but little agricultural surplus.

In protectionist theory there was nothing to stop the Americans importing molasses from the French colonies, but obviously this trade alarmed the British planters and merchants. They saw the Americans taking their currency to buy molasses from their greatest rivals, and this was an extremely serious problem in view of the chronic shortage of coinage in all colonies. Any balance would be taken in credit notes, redeemable in London, with which the Americans hoped to pay for their necessary imports. The West Indians, supported by English shippers and refiners, protested, and as a result the government passed the Molasses Act 1733, imposing a heavy charge of 6d per gallon on foreign molasses imported into America.

The Americans of course resented this imposition, and became increasingly bitter about the pampered and privileged West Indian colonists. In fact the Act, although a technical victory for the West Indians, had very little effect, as it was not enforced, since the Americans were able to use their fast ships and heavily indented coastline to smuggle in French molasses. The British government only took serious steps against this trade when it was found to be continuing unabated during wars with France, and that French colonies were being sustained by American supplies, often delivered directly or through the Dutch entrepôts.

It is significant that when the British government decided to collect a revenue from colonial trade to pay for colonial defence, the Sugar Act of 1764 actually reduced the duties on molasses from 6*d* to 3*d* a gallon, but proposed to collect them with the help of improved customs services and the navy. This measure caused a great panic in the northern colonies. Constitutional objections were raised, and John Adams, a colonial leader, admitted 'that molasses was an essential ingredient in American independence'.

The imperial system had proved itself incapable of supporting the rapidly growing American economy. The population of the American colonies doubled every twenty-five years in the eighteenth century, their commercial network became more extensive, their imports increased and the problem of paying for them grew more acute. One of the underlying causes of the differences between England and the American colonies can be found in this economic impasse.

The southern American colonies fitted more easily into the fashionable concept of colonies. Virginia and Maryland were quickly established as plantation colonies, producing a valuable staple in tobacco, and increasingly using a slave labour force. Their only problem was to find enough new land to which the labour force could be moved in order to grow more tobacco, and this issue eventually brought these colonists too into collision with the home government, which wanted to restrain any westward expansion in order to avoid expensive clashes with Indians or the French. Virginian planters had a tendency towards overproduction, which had a bad effect on prices, but they became aware of this during the century, and the planter assembly attempted to ban the import of slaves into the colony before the American Revolution in an attempt to limit tobacco growing. The British government refused to accept such an outrageous idea, since this would have hit the vital British interest of slaving, and would have forced up tobacco prices in England, making the re-export trade less valuable. The encouragement of British maritime strength was put forward as an argument for the trade continuing (**43, 46**).

The Carolinas were the fastest developing of the American colonies in the eighteenth century. They had plantations in the tidewater areas, but further inland the economy was more that of

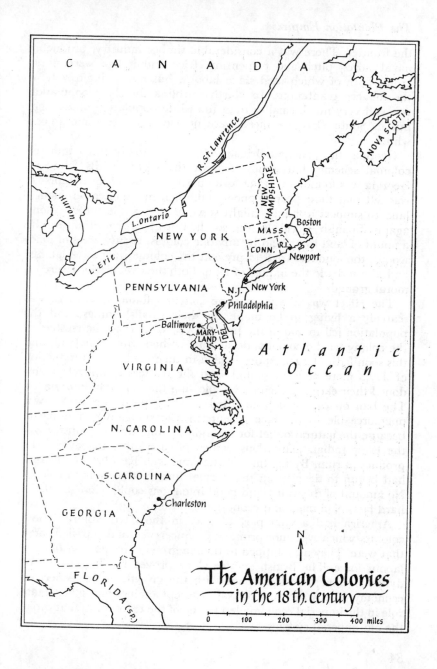

The American Colonies in the 18th century

CANADA

L. Huron

L. Ontario

L. Erie

R. St. Lawrence

NOVA SCOTIA

NEW YORK

NEW HAMPSHIRE

MASS.

CONN. R.I.

Boston

Newport

N.J.

New York

PENNSYLVANIA

Philadelphia

Baltimore

MARY-LAND

VIRGINIA

Atlantic Ocean

N. CAROLINA

S. CAROLINA

GEORGIA

Charleston

FLORIDA (SP.)

N

0   100   200   300   400 miles

the frontier. There was a considerable timber industry, producing naval stores, pitch and turpentine. Rice and indigo were staple crops, both of which used slave labour, but not so intensively as the tobacco plantations. In North Carolina the slave population was still very much smaller than the white population of 200,000, but in South Carolina there were 95,000 slaves to some 40,000 whites.

Georgia, the youngest British colony, eventually fitted into the colonial scheme, but almost against the wishes of its founders. Georgia was founded in 1732 as a charitable colony for debtors. It was felt that these people, once established in America on enough land to support a family, might serve as a valuable buffer colony against Spanish Florida to the south. But apart from limiting the amount of land to be held by any one colonist to fifty acres of pine-woods, the founders tried to prevent the colony using slave labour, and also forbade the import of rum. Both these regulations were on moral grounds.

The effect was disastrous. The colonists found that there was scarcely a living to be made on their small-holdings, and the population fell to 500 in the first ten years. In 1750 the trustees of the colony let the colonists do as they wished with their land, and this soon led to larger estates, which in turn made the introduction of slaves more or less essential, and the trustees completely abandoned their earlier principles by allowing the importation of slaves. The ban on rum had been lifted in 1743, partly because it was unenforceable in the face of enterprising smuggling, and partly because the natural outlet for Georgia's young timber industry was the West Indian plantations, which often wanted to pay for the product in rum. By the time of the American Revolution, Georgia had begun to develop on the normal lines of a plantation colony. No amount of theorising and good intentions could win against the hard facts of climate and economic conditions (**43**).

America had a vital part to play in the slave empire. Those colonies which were not primary producers fed and supplied those that were. They also shipped to them a growing proportion of their labour force. The British empire alone proved not big enough or dynamic enough to keep pace with the growth of the American economy. The Americans' refusal to accept a minor and subordinate role in the imperial economy led to one of the revolutions that broke the old imperial systems.

6 The Empire as a Success

'Sugar, Mr Speaker,' said the elder Pitt in the House of Commons in 1759, 'who will laugh at sugar now?' Indeed, by the middle of the eighteenth century the plantation colonies were no laughing matter to the governments of France and England. They had become pre-eminently important to the economies of both countries, whose industrial and commercial prosperity depended very largely upon their overseas possessions.

Although economists later in the eighteenth century were to attack the concept of the profitability of the colonial empire, in the middle of the century the belief in them as a major source of national wealth was unchallenged. A pamphlet of 1749 declared: 'The most approved Judges of the Commercial Interests of these Kingdoms have ever been of the opinion that our West-India and Africa Trades are the most nationally beneficial of any we carry on' [doc. 24]. As we have seen, the relationship between the mother countries and the colonies was based on commerce, and this explains the especially high regard in which the Caribbean colonies were held in London and Versailles [docs 24, 25].

Figures show the importance of colonial trade in the British and French economies. In 1700 the two-way trade between England and the West Indies constituted 7 per cent of the total English trade, while the two-way trade between England and the American colonies at that time was only 6 per cent of the total.

The boom years for the plantation colonies were roughly 1714–73. The trade figures for these years have been worked out in some detail, and are given below as percentages:

	%		%
Total British imports	100	Total British exports	100
Imports from West Indies	20·5	Exports to West Indies	6·2
Imports from American colonies	11·3	Exports to American colonies	9·6
Imports from Africa	0·5	Exports to Africa	2·1

	%
Total British trade	100
Total West Indies trade	12
Total American trade	10·2
Total African trade	1·4

These figures are somewhat deceptive, as the import trade from Africa, for example, would be better reflected in the slave trade, and this is shown as part of the West Indian import figure, since the slaves were usually exchanged for plantation goods. We should also note that during this period the exports to America were greater than those to the West Indies, and this was to be significant when the manufacturers of the Industrial Revolution became more and more market-conscious and also gained a share of political power in both England and France.

This shift in the proportion of imports and exports is shown even more markedly if one looks at the end of the period to 1773.

1773	% of total British imports
British imports ex W.I. colonies	24·8
British imports ex American colonies	12·5
	% of total British exports
British exports to W.I. colonies	8·6
British exports to American colonies	16·1
	% of total British trade
Total W.I. trade	15·5
Total American trade	14·5

These figures suggest that the American trading connections with both the British and the French colonies in the Caribbean had built up the young American economy to such an extent that the American colonies could become a major market for British goods (3).

French trade figures suggest the same pattern. By the middle of the century up to a third of French trade was colonial, and the great advance in production in the French islands was from 1763 until the Revolution. Immediately before the Revolution the French sugar colonies were sending home annually 100,000 tons of sugar, compared with 90,000 tons from the British plantations. The greater output and lower production costs of French plantations in this period gave French merchants control of the European market, and more than two-fifths of French exports consisted of re-exported colonial produce, mostly sugar. This more than accounted for the favourable balance of trade enjoyed by France, which in turn generated the national prosperity reflected in all-round commercial and industrial advance.

This commercial activity was first reflected in those ports in the mother countries concerned with colonial trade. London remained the commercial capital of England, even if it lost the leadership of the slave trade to Liverpool and was challenged in the direct trade with the West Indies by Bristol. In 1794, between May and October, there were 433 West India ships in the Thames, bringing 122,000 hogsheads of sugar. The sugar and other exotic cargoes gave rise to a great deal of theft. One estimate put the number of thieves in the docks at 11,000. They had the delightful nicknames of mudlarks, scuffle-hunters and light horsemen, and it was largely to combat their pilfering that the West India merchants helped establish the River Police in 1798, and in the following year secured an Act of Parliament to build the West India Docks. A capital of £1,380,000 was raised, and docks were built on a 295-acre site on the Isle of Dogs, with accommodation for 600 vessels of 250–500 tons, the size of ship used on the Caribbean run. The docks were surrounded by a wall and sentries were mounted. All this activity demonstrates the very real value of West India trade in the capital at the end of the century (**18**).

Whereas colonial trade played an important part in London's commerce, it was the whole basis of Bristol's. The west country port lost the lead in slaving to Liverpool during the century, and came to rely on direct trade with the colonies. A wide range of goods, mostly produced in the Midlands, was exported, and in return Bristol imported raw sugar for its refineries, molasses for local distilleries, and tobacco. There were very close links between Bristol merchant houses and the colonies, and during the century more and more merchants became shipowners and planters, and in some cases planters became merchants. Bristol completed a Floating Harbour in 1809 at the cost of £600,000, and the high style of Bristol merchant houses, their country estates and their willingness to invest show the profitability of colonial trade (**18, 27**).

Liverpool was created by the African and West Indian trades. It had the advantage of the developing industrial hinterland of Lancashire, and by serving as a link between this and the colonies, Liverpool rose to become England's second port. Even more surprising a reflection on the value of colonial trade was White-haven's emergence as a major port based on the tobacco trade, a status it held for a great part of the century (**78**).

After the Act of Union in 1707 it was possible for Scottish merchants to take part in colonial trade. As a result Glasgow immediately prospered, using the north of England as its hinterland and being the terminus of a safe, short sea route to Virginia. By mid-century Glasgow's 'Tobacco Lords' were importing 30 million pounds of tobacco per annum, securing supplies by controlling stores in up-country Virginia, and from 1740 re-exporting to the United General Farms of France.

In France, the west coast ports received a similar boost from the French plantation colonies. Nantes, La Rochelle and Bordeaux were all intimately connected with the French West Indies, import-ing and refining sugar, and exporting manufactured goods and much more food, wine and livestock than their English counterparts, since French North America was unable to fill this rôle.

The shipbuilding industries in Britain and in the American colonies received an obvious stimulus from this traffic. In the seventy-five years up to 1770, the number of ships employed in colonial trade increased five times, and probably involved as many as three thousand vessels.

Since all manufactured goods had to be imported by the colonies, there was an obvious link between the prosperity of the colonies and the development of industries in the mother countries. The argu-ments of the protectionists in this respect were true for the first stages of industrial growth. An English pamphlet claimed: 'Five hundred thousand negroes are constantly clad by the clothiers of Yorkshire and Wiltshire. London, Birmingham, Bristol and Carron supply alike the mill-work, the nails, the hoes, the tools, the utensils of domestic life and the implements of husbandry' (**3**).

The plantation colonies themselves provided the best evidence of the success of the system. The wealth of the British Caribbean colonies was largely in the hands of absentee owners, and these families established a reputation for ostentatious expenditure in England, on houses, servants, hospitality and political advancement. There is the well-known story of George III meeting a Jamaican absentee-planter and his enormous retinue on the road near Wey-mouth, and turning to the younger Pitt to say 'Sugar, sugar, hey?—all that sugar! How are the duties, hey, Pitt, how are the duties?' (**39**).

Even Adam Smith, a devastating critic of the old imperial system, wrote: 'The profits of a sugar plantation in any one of our West Indian colonies are generally much greater than those of any other cultivation that is known either in Europe or America.' And by 1764 much of these profits were finding their way to England. It was claimed that British investment in the sugar colonies had reached between £4 million and £5 million.

By the middle of the eighteenth century the plantation colonies had reached a peak of wealth and prestige, but they were also on the verge of outliving their economic usefulness. This decline will be examined in the second half of the book. Enough at this stage to notice that the colonial powers of northern Europe felt themselves to be superior largely because they possessed colonies. Thus the great French minister, Choiseul, himself connected with the West Indies, wrote: 'The House of Austria, Russia, the King of Prussia, are only second-rate states, since they can make war only when they are subsidised by the commercial powers.' The commercial powers were convinced that their prosperity was linked with their plantation colonies.

Part Two

FORCES OF CHANGE

7 Clash of Interests

Although the British plantation empire in mid-eighteenth century was so highly prized and seemed so firmly established, a varied and articulate body of opinion opposed to the system grew up during the century. When the plantation system began to prove less than efficient there were many groups ready to attack it on economic, strategic, financial and humanitarian grounds, while its defenders were disunited and to some extent uncertain.

Generally speaking, the 'Establishment' was in favour of the colonies. The king, if he aired views at all, was generally in favour of his possessions being as wide as possible. George III held West Indian colonies in especially high regard. In 1782 he wrote: 'I would wish if possible to get rid of Gibraltar, and to have as much possession in the West Indies as possible.' Three years previously he had written: 'Our West Indian islands must be defended even at the risk of an invasion of this island. If we lose our sugar islands it will be impossible to raise money to continue the war.' His anxiety to hold the American colonies in submission, by force when necessary, is well known.

For various reasons most of the leading ministers favoured the colonies during the eighteenth century. The elder Pitt was the great architect of an American empire; Newcastle was deeply concerned with trade, as is shown by his claim in the year before his death that he had always tried to 'contribute all that was in my power to the encouragement and extension of the trade and commerce of these kingdoms'; Lord North acted as the tool of the king in hanging on to the American colonies for as long as possible; the younger Pitt, even though professing to follow the teachings of Adam Smith, devoted much of his war effort to weakening France by annexing Caribbean islands.

The government saw the colonies as fundamentally important to the economy, as a valuable source of customs revenue, as strategically vital, and, not least, as a source of patronage. Political support had to be paid for in offices and sinecures, and the colonies were a rich preserve. James Mill put his finger on this aspect in the next century when he called the empire 'a vast system of outdoor relief for the upper classes'.

In both houses of Parliament there was strong support for the West Indian colonies. This was so constant, and the West Indian plantation colonies were so regularly favoured against, for example, the mainland colonies, that it was widely believed that there was a powerful West India lobby in Parliament. The simple assumption was that the West Indian absentee planters returned to England and purchased parliamentary seats, partly for social prestige and partly to protect their colonial interests. The American colonists were always referring to 'pampered creoles' and a pamphlet put out by Boston merchants in 1764 after the passing of the Sugar Act claimed:

> This act was procured by the interests of the West India planters, with no other view than to enrich themselves, by obliging the northern Colonies to take their whole supply from them; and they still endeavour the continuance of it under a pretence, that they can supply Great Britain and all her Colonies with West India goods, which is perfectly chimerical.

Professor Namier investigated the structure of Parliament in the middle of the century. On the question of whether there was a powerful West Indian parliamentary *bloc*, he wrote:

> Only those should be counted who were born in the West Indies, had spent there part of their lives, had been a member of a West Indian assembly or Council, or had held office in one of the islands; and of these I find only thirteen in the House of Commons elected in 1761.

He goes on to say that

> even counting those who might be described as the 'outer ring' of the West Indian group, it is doubtful whether the figure of forty can be reached—I know of only eight or nine members in 1761 whose connections with, or interests in, the West Indies qualify them for being placed in that 'outer ring'.

He concluded that

> what in reality helped the West Indians much more than some twenty votes in a house of 558, was that their commercial demands were in accordance with the mercantilist doctrines of trade, which at that time were universally accepted and punctiliously adhered to in Great Britain (**51**).

Professor Burn has made the point that a small, united group would have been influential beyond its numbers in a House of Commons in which the two-party system did not operate. The 'inner ring' no doubt generated the pro-colonial feeling, but the great majority of members supported it, partly because the idea of an empire came to be connected with national greatness, and partly because defence of the colonies came to be considered as a defence of property. The elder Pitt went on record as saying that 'he should ever consider the sugar colonies as the landed interest of this kingdom, and it was a barbarism to consider them otherwise' (2).

Merchants made up a sizeable group in the House of Commons, and connections between the City of London, the Government and Parliament were always of the closest. As a result, the West Indian cause was, with that of the East India Company, cherished. To quote Professor Namier again on this difficult point of why one aspect of national life should receive what appears to be more than its due attention:

> Though the State primarily belongs to the owners of the land, it is the circulating part of the nation which is most directly concerned with government; and governments, as all human institutions, are influenced and shaped by those who are willing to work and pay for them, i.e. those who need them most ... consequently trade is at all times much more the subject of legislation than agriculture (51).

The West Indian pressure group certainly existed, and not only as an active voting group in Parliament. In each of the great sea ports connected with the colonies there were vociferous and influential West Indian associations. In London there was the Society of West India Merchants and the Planters' Club, which combined to form the Meeting of West Indian Planters and Merchants [**doc. 27**]. These had separate constitutions, but very similar memberships. The Admiralty corresponded with the former during wars to arrange the convoys, and when the younger Pitt wanted to alter the duties on East Indian sugar he met the Standing Committee of the latter to explain his ideas, and it was significant that he modified his scheme after this discussion. This combination of planters and merchants finally came together as the West India Committee. These organisations could exert considerable political pressure when they believed their interests were at stake, and they always stereotyped the colonial system [**doc. 28**]. In addition, each island colony also had its Agent in England to watch over its interests (**67**).

The French West India interest was never so influential, since the interests of the planters and the merchants did not coincide either over exports or imports. The planters were for the most part resident, and the merchants of Nantes and La Rochelle were geographically out of touch with affairs in the capital, even though they had regular contact with the government through the *Bureau de Commerce*. Finally, of course, there was no equivalent of Parliament in France until the Revolution, and then, as we shall see, the attitude towards the colonies was ambivalent.

The Navy always had a keen interest in the colonies and in the slave trade, since it regarded them as the nurseries of seamen and also one of its own *raisons d'être*. Nelson had his own special interest in the colonies, since his wife was a colonial, and so his comment is probably an emphatic version of the naval view:

> I was bred in the good old school, and taught to appreciate the value of our West Indian possessions, and neither in the field nor the Senate shall their just rights be infringed while I have an arm to fight in their defence, or a tongue to launch my voice against the damnable doctrine of Wilberforce and his hypocritical allies (**3**).

When there was a threat to sugar prices or to the slave trade or to the very institution of slavery, the various interested groups could be counted on to rally, and their voice would be heard. When the struggle for abolition of the slave trade was reaching a climax in 1791, the West Indian colonists quickly raised £10,000 to fight any further Bills.

So much for the groups in favour of the colonies; but there were also powerful voices opposed to them. During the eighteenth century the basic attitude towards colonies and slavery underwent a marked change. Economists began to preach the gospel of free trade, advocating the abandonment of imperial preferences. Accompanying this major change, there was the growing Radicalism in politics and the seeds of humanitarianism in all walks of life. These trends will be examined in more detail in a later chapter.

Both before and after the American Revolution, there were voices within the empire that felt the West Indians had too many privileges. The Americans regarded the West Indian political influence with outraged suspicion, and they were convinced that the resulting economic advantages were at their expense. In the second half of the century, the economic interests of the East were advanced in Parliament and in the City. The growth of sugar agriculture in the East, which was based on very low wages but not on slavery, gave the eastern merchants the chance to attack the slave trade, while at the same time being able to point to the greater markets of the east (3).

New economic groups were finding the system of protection confining from the point of view of both imports and exports. The growing industrial voice was normally in favour of markets as wide as possible.

On the import side we find the same story. Even industries that had grown up under the protective system—refiners, distillers—and the grocers, both wholesalers and retailers, discovered that the demand they had created could not be filled fully by the British plantation colonies alone. The distillers found they were not getting the molasses they wanted in face of competition from North America, while the refiners were constantly trying to get foreign sugar allowed on the British market legally. A pamphlet of 1784 put it bluntly: 'If the British plantations cannot, or will not, afford sugar, etc., plenty and cheap enough the French, Dutch, and Portuguese do, and will' (3).

A final and important group concerned with imports were the re-exporters. They saw their European markets being challenged and finally seized by French rivals, using the vast sugar estates of St Domingue. As the British sugar producers were content with a relatively fixed production and a protected market, they were increasingly open to criticism as they fell further and further behind demand.

Throughout the century there was a strong body of isolationist opinion in Britain. This can be called the 'Little Englander' outlook, and was to be found even amongst ministers and members of Parliament. Naturally this attitude tended to increase with the cost of colonial wars. It is to be found in the tendency to avoid acquiring valuable colonial territories as a result of wars, since this would inevitably make the losers want revenge, so causing further wars. As the cost of colonial wars soared, many British taxpayers began to think critically of the colonies themselves.

In the course of the eighteenth century, the voices raised against the old colonial system became both more numerous and more articulate. At the same time the British sugar interest became more desperate in the face of its falling profitability and therefore more determined not to give way at any point in the defence of its advantageous position. The balance between the defenders and the critics of the colonial system constantly altered as a result of the American, French and Industrial revolutions. It was not a question of the old colonial system ending at some point in time, and being replaced by a new system based on commerce. The firmly entrenched plantation and slavery interests were not to surrender so easily (52).

8 Colonial Warfare

With two aggressive countries, such as England and France, establishing similar and neighbouring colonies in the Caribbean and both protecting their wealth in rigidly protectionist ways, it was almost inevitable that the Caribbean should become a regular theatre of war in the eighteenth century.

Although there was fighting in that sea or on the islands in every war during the century, the sugar colonies were never the actual cause of wars between the two countries. The eighteenth century wars were fought to preserve a balance of power in Europe, and this struggle went on all over the world, naturally including West Africa and the West Indies. Bryan Edwards, the eighteenth-century West Indian historian, summed it up: 'Thither the combatants repair, as to an arena' (**12**). Professor Harlow referred to the colonial warfare as only a 'by-product' of the major struggle in Europe (**52**).

A change in emphasis from a continental to a maritime strategy is a feature of the eighteenth century (**71**). British and French fleets were sent out from Europe, even at the risk of weakening home defences dangerously, and troops were diverted from North America to defend the islands.

The struggle with France in the Caribbean during the eighteenth century grew out of England's successful efforts to attack, exploit and dismember the Spanish empire in the New World. By 1714, Spain and its empire were tottering, but the French Bourbons were on the throne of Spain, and England feared that France might gain an undue share of Spanish imperial trade.

By the Treaty of Utrecht in 1714 England secured the famous *Asiento*, the licence to supply 4,800 slaves per annum to the Spanish colonies, with the right to send an annual ship to trade at the Portobello fair. The South Sea Company, which was formed to organise this trade, was in fact more concerned with government finance and allowed its commercial interests to decline. However, under the cover of the Company, British merchants opened up various illegal trades to the desperate Spanish colonists, who were not being supplied by Spain (**54**). This led to a series of incidents with the Spanish *guarda costas* over the right of search at sea. In addition there were other problems—such as the interminable logwood claims on the Honduras mainland and frontier demarcation claims between Georgia and Florida—and the situation built up to a war in 1739. The most celebrated—and very possibly bogus—incident gave the war its odd name of Jenkins' Ear. It was the first war fought expressly for West Indian ends, and it began in a burst of national enthusiasm. 'Take and Hold' was the cry (**31**).

The war was surprisingly unrewarding. The soldiers and sailors had not mastered West Indian conditions, and there were many complete fiascos. France, under Fleury, stayed out more by luck than good management until 1744, when the French were no longer prepared to stand by and watch this assault on the Spanish empire by their main rivals, especially since their legitimate trade to the Spanish colonies through Cadiz was being effectively cut off. By the Treaty of Aix-la-Chapelle in 1748 the *Asiento* was withdrawn and the Caribbean *status quo* was restored. But France had declared its hand, and the confrontation between the two countries was a reality.

AIMS

Even when a maritime and colonial war had been decided upon, the specific aims of Caribbean warfare remained unclear, indeed often conflicting. In the first place the overall British interest might conflict with West Indian interests. The former might well be served by the conquest of an enemy colony, while the latter would be horrified at the idea of new sugar lands gaining entry into the protected English market [**doc. 21**]. Secondly, each colony thought primarily of its own security and interests. A regiment and a section of the fleet was demanded by each colony to protect it against enemy raids. At the same time, destructive raids on enemy islands' mills and canefields or slave raids were the only projects that colonists on either side actively supported [**doc. 20**].

British ministers regarded Caribbean islands as comparatively easy to capture and valuable as bargaining counters at the subsequent treaties. As a result, it was rare for Caribbean colonies to change hands permanently, in spite of being regularly captured and occupied. To avoid tensions the islands, whose ownership was contested—St Lucia, St Vincent, Dominica and Tobago—were declared 'neutral', although this seems to have been a fiction, since they remained effectively French and no proper evacuation seems to have been carried out.

It can be seen that, to some extent, the aims of the British government in the Caribbean theatre—the acquisition of bargaining counters—coincided with the aims of the colonists, namely the capture of enemy colonies without permanent annexation. The differences between the two attitudes arose over the use of the captured colonies during the period of occupation, when the government saw the opportunity of increasing imports, assisted by the private enterprise of the slavers, while the colonists saw capital and labour being poured into islands that would become very real rivals for the home market (**31**).

In addition there were certain strategic aims in the Caribbean. St Lucia was to the windward of Martinique, and so was able to dominate this, the leading French island in the area. It was also the essential link between the French and the British Windward islands. For this reason St Lucia was always a major demand by French negotiators, and played an important part in the 1763 peace talks. The 'neutral' island of Dominica lies directly between Guadeloupe and Martinique, and both the French and the British saw its strategic value in the likely event of another war.

During wars such bases became more significant because of the practice of employing privateers and naval auxiliaries. The French, usually the weaker naval power in the area, played havoc with British trade in this way, and after 1748 British West Indian colonists became increasingly more concerned, to the extent that eventually they were prepared to see the main privateering bases permanently annexed.

Privateers were by no means the only seamen interested in commerce-raiding. The prize money system in the Royal Navy gave half the value of a captured enemy ship to the officers and crew. The division was, not surprisingly, monstrously in favour of the admirals and senior officers, ensuring that commerce-raiding and the seizing of enemy harbours became ends in themselves, possibly at the expense of more important but less lucrative

51

strategic aims. Admiral Vernon, who achieved little against Spain in the War of Jenkins' Ear, nevertheless returned a very wealthy man—'his laurels tipped with gold'. Rodney, the most celebrated admiral in the Caribbean, was also the most greedy. His greatest coup, the capture and occupation of the Dutch 'free port' of St Eustatius during the War of American Independence, led to an exploitation of the prize so thorough that the security of all the British West Indies was hazarded.

Trade provided other war aims, both defensive and offensive. Defoe referred to commerce and naval power as 'twins born together, not to live asunder'. In the first place British colonial trade had to be protected by convoys, while enemy trade had to be destroyed as far as possible by interception or blockade. In addition the Navy was used during wars to open up new trading areas in the Caribbean. Thus traders were escorted to the coast of the enemy colonies, and attacks were planned where merchants could follow up, as in the 1748 attack on St Domingue. Vernon was a great believer in such operations. In his raids on Portobello and Chagres in 1739 he destroyed the forts so that an English warship could always cover English merchants trading there.

The slavers were particularly enthusiastic about such projects. Both French and Spanish colonies were chronically underprovided with slaves, and British, Dutch and American slavers were more than ready to supply them. Thus slaves were poured into Guadeloupe, Martinique and Havana when they were occupied. To support this activity, complementary raids were made on enemy stations on the West African coast. Keppel took a strong force to the French island colony of Gorée in 1758, and the capture of that colony and Senegal might well have crippled the French West Indies permanently, if they had been retained at the peace.

METHODS

With the aims of Caribbean warfare being so confused, government versus colonists, island versus island, and admirals for themselves, it is not surprising that the resulting achievements were disappointing. Furthermore, the methods of achieving these aims were often extraordinarily inefficient (**31**).

The Caribbean wars were primarily naval. Command of the sea

was essential to achieve any of the aims mentioned. With this, convoys could be brought through, enemy trade could be confined, enemy colonies could be raided or occupied, and friendly colonies could be defended. The problem was to achieve any degree of permanent control with wooden sailing ships and poor communications.

The British and French had opposing theories about maintaining naval forces in the Caribbean. The British early decided on permanent squadrons, based in Jamaica from 1704, and in Antigua from 1743. Port Royal in Jamaica and English Harbour in Antigua provided some dockyard facilities and stores. The former squadron could protect Jamaica and harass the Spanish colonies, while the latter was responsible for the Leeward Islands and the French colonies.

The French, on the other hand, sent out fleets from Europe to wage a campaign in the Caribbean during the short season, April to July, before hurricanes were to be expected. Then sailing ships had to shelter, return to Europe or sail to North America. The French did not base a permanent squadron in Martinique until 1784.

The British system may seem superior, but in fact its advantages were not so obvious. The British bases were unhealthy spots (Nelson called English Harbour 'a vile hole'), dockyard facilities were poor, crews were usually below strength, and the ships soon became unseaworthy in the Caribbean because of shipworm, a problem not solved until the introduction of copper-sheathing towards the end of the century. The French fleets, on the other hand, arrived in the West Indies at nearly full strength, and with an element of surprise. This depended, however, on the ability of the French to get a fleet through the British wartime blockade of the European coastline, which became steadily more efficient during the century. If the French government favoured a continental policy, the inevitable economies would fall upon the navy, which would be kept in port since the Caribbean campaign was regarded as of peripheral importance.

As a result, the British held command of the sea in most of the eighteenth century wars, with the notable exception of the War of American Independence, when for once the French were able to fight on equal terms without European military commitments. It was usually the British who were best able to execute their aims.

Apart from fleet actions and privateering, there were occasional attempts at combined operations, but these were rarely successful. Troops had to be in action immediately on arrival in the West Indies, before the inevitable effects of fever and rum—'Captain Punch'—took their toll. Bad water and the climate added to the problems for European troops. Local men might have been immune, but they were untrained and unwilling to leave their own islands open to attack. Troops stationed in the islands were in part paid for by the individual assemblies, which obstructed attempts to base an offensive force on them, since successful expeditions might result in conquests they did not want.

The island militias could make some mild defensive show, although there are no examples of desperate local defences [**doc. 22**]. The forces were small, because the white population was small in the islands, and no system of taxing plantations that did not support Europeans—known as Deficiency Taxes—seems to have had effect. The primary function of the militias was to protect the white population against slave risings. Because of this fear, powers rarely considered either arming their own negroes or encouraging the enemy's negroes to rise on their behalf.

Apart from a few spectacular battles and campaigns, the pattern of West Indian warfare was pettily destructive. The norm was constant privateering and frequent raids. Both activities were especially favoured by the French, who had the larger white population. They were designed to inflict the maximum destruction, since raided islands took anything up to twenty years to recover fully. French expertise in these two fields meant that warfare in the West Indies was by no means as one-sided as an account of captured islands would suggest.

9 The Seven Years War

The major confrontation between England and France during the eighteenth century was the Seven Years War from 1756–63. In the war the two powers fought one another all over the world, in Europe, in India, in North America, in Africa, and, inevitably, in the Caribbean (**31**). The Seven Years War is typical of the warfare described in the last chapter, except that during the war popular opinion in England began to demand the expulsion of the French from the whole of the American hemisphere.

The French were able to make a major effort in the Caribbean during this war. As a result of the capture of Minorca in 1756 the Mediterranean was virtually closed to English fleets, leaving French ships available to counter the English in the West Indies. Four major naval expeditions were sent out during the war, and their aims were not only defensive. They were to disrupt English trade and, if possible, to annex Jamaica.

The capture of Minorca opened large-scale hostilities in the Caribbean. Already privateering and raids had begun, and colonists of both countries clamoured for ships and troops. Chatham, advised by Beckford, the enormously wealthy Jamaican planter, decided to take Martinique as a suitable bargaining counter for the return of Minorca at the peace. This was a shrewd calculation. The French Minister of Marine, who was responsible for the colonies, asked: 'Is it not humiliating to think the loss of Martinique will transfer to them a trade worth 70 million livres, or two-thirds of the interest of their national debt?'

The attack on Martinique in 1759 was a failure, but the second French island of Guadeloupe was taken by the same expedition. As usual there was little attempt to defend the island, since it was felt this was futile and liable to provoke destruction on a large scale. In this instance the French surrendered with almost indecent haste, as the terms offered them were extremely generous—in the eyes of British colonists disastrously so. The occupying force realised that

C

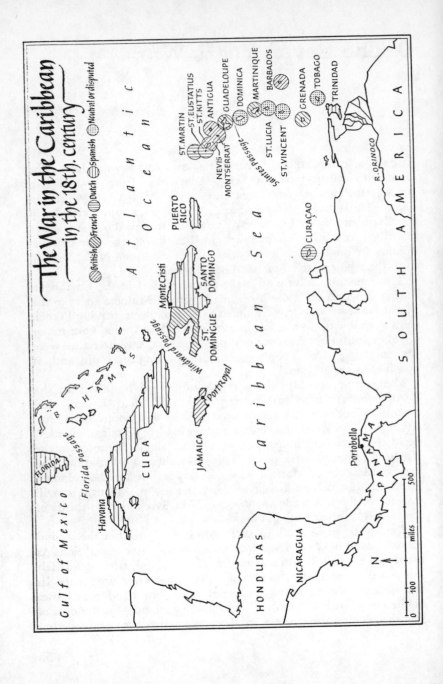

The War in the Caribbean in the 18th century

British   French   Dutch   Spanish   Neutral or disputed

the large white population, once alienated, would be difficult to control and at the same time appreciated that the island was certain to be returned to the French at the peace, so making any transfer of property pointless. Thus the property rights, religious practices and the legal position of the French planters were preserved: no new taxes were imposed: and British would-be land purchasers were kept out. In addition, the French planters were allowed to import slaves from British and American slavers and to export sugar to Britain, as if they were full members of the imperial system.

The effect of these measures was just what the British planters had feared. The price of sugar on the London market fell sharply: the cost of food and lumber from North America soared, as American traders rushed to sell in the best market, and one where molasses were plentiful and cheap: and slaves became more expensive, sometimes almost unobtainable in British colonies, as they were diverted to Guadeloupe.

By the end of 1760, the 'Neutral' Islands and Grenada had also been captured by the British, although it should be noted that these islands were not offered the generous terms given to the colonists of Guadeloupe. Technically the French had no right to be in the 'Neutral' Islands, and Rodney assumed that these islands would not be handed back to the French at the peace, which, in fact, now seemed imminent, as Chatham's effective strategy had produced victories in India, Gorée and Canada. France was ready to negotiate, and England responded when Spain renewed the Family Compact with France in 1761, since this might well place the country at a naval disadvantage, as well as dangerously overextending her Caribbean forces.

Chatham had already opened peace negotiations in October 1761, when he was dismissed, to be replaced by the much more pacific Bute and the Duke of Bedford, a 'Little Englander' *par excellence*, who wanted nothing in the treaty likely to antagonise France into further wars of revenge.

Talk of peace from 1760 launched the famous controversy as to whether it was more desirable to retain Canada or Guadeloupe at the peace. In terms of trade and current estimation, there was no doubt in French or English minds—Guadeloupe was infinitely the more desirable. Furthermore, if the key positions of Louisburg and Newfoundland were kept in British hands, the French in Canada could be effectively contained, while their continued presence there would have the additional side benefit of keeping the American colonists dependent and loyal. Canada's value was hypothetical, although not so minimal as Voltaire's 'quelques arpents de neige vers le Canada' suggests [**doc. 23**] [E.H.D. X].

But naturally this argument was not accepted by the British planters in the West Indies or by their vociferous pressure groups in London. They feared the rivalry of Guadeloupe within the empire, and screamed for its return to France, implying thereby the retention of Canada. In fact there was little doubt in 1761 that Canada would be retained simply for strategic reasons, and that Chatham had made Canada and the fisheries his basic demand by April 1761. The huge potential of North America was at last being recognised, but so feared was the West Indian voice that this decision was at once attributed to the sinister influence of the 'creoles'. Chatham had a point when he said in Parliament: 'Some are for keeping Canada: some, Guadeloupe. Who will tell me which I will be hanged for not keeping?'

If a peace had been concluded in 1761, there would have been little problem. Choiseul wanted Guadeloupe back, Chatham wanted Canada. But peace was not made then. In the following two years, British naval superiority led to further sweeping conquests. In 1762 Martinique itself and the remaining French islands in the group were captured; then Havana was seized from Spain. The ministers who had wanted a simple negotiated peace were horrified. They were actually relieved that news of Anson's capture of Manila came too late to influence the treaty.

There had been no real doubt about Canada being retained in preference to Guadeloupe, but it became a much more nicely balanced problem when virtually the whole of the French West Indies was a possible acquisition. With so many conquests, something would have to be retained. Even the West Indians had come round to accepting this, and Professor Pares has shown that the West Indian attitude to new acquisitions was much 'softer' in the 1760s than it had been in the 1740s (**31**). He suggested that the severe damage done to colonial shipping by French privateers based on Martinique, and fear of raids had persuaded the planters. In any event, congratulatory addresses were sent to the king on the capture of Martinique. The Grand Jury of Barbados asked for the island to be permanently annexed; the Legislature of Antigua advocated the retention of both Martinique and Guadeloupe. Rodney summarised their predicament succinctly in 1762: 'The planters are divided between avarice and fear ... the example of this war has taught them a lesson, which I fancy they will never forget.'

The point was all too clear. The British fleet had saved the British sugar colonies, and it had enabled all the French colonies, except St Domingue, to be captured. The influential West Indian 'voice' could be ignored. Canada was kept, but not to accomodate the planters, and all the key French islands, including potentially dangerous St Lucia, were handed back to the French in spite of colonial demands to the contrary. Professor Burn concluded that 'the West Indian interest was no more able to determine the terms of peace than it had been able to determine the conduct of the war (2). One has to reject Dr Eric Williams's ingenious argument that 'Canada and Florida were retained precisely because they were *less* valuable' (3).

As important a statesman as Shelburne was already criticising the West Indian sugar colonies, claiming they tended to 'weaken and depopulate the mother country'. Economists and manufacturers were setting the cost of defending the colonies against their comparative inefficiency. As markets they were hopelessly inadequate and already compared unfavourably with North America in this respect. The Seven Years War as a struggle for Empire exposed the fact that the West Indies were no longer to be regarded as 'the brightest jewels in His Majesty's crown'.

In the event, the Treaty of Paris produced very little change in the West Indian situation. Bute demanded and got the whole of North America as far as the left bank of the Mississippi, and took Grenada and the 'Neutral' Islands, with the exception of St Lucia, which the French kept in return for navigation concessions on the Mississippi. The French position, based on St Domingue, Guadeloupe and Martinique, was virtually unchanged, and they got back their West African slaving stations. It was believed that this delicate situation could always be maintained by the navy, while Britain now had a defensible land frontier on the continent of North America.

Professor Pares concluded that the settlement 'combined the greatest possible gain for England with the smallest loss for France' (31). Bute he saw as following Chatham in that he 'conquered in the islands in order to annex on the continent'. John Wilkes's famous description of the treaty as being 'like the peace of God—it passeth all understanding' is memorable but unfair.

10 The American Revolution

The British had achieved most of their American aims in the Seven Years War, but to do this they had left the French and the Spanish in their former powerful positions in the Caribbean. In addition, the Dutch, although scarcely an imperial power in the New World, maintained a dominant commercial position through their 'free port' system on the islands of St Eustatius, St Martin and Curaçao. The British were prepared to share the Caribbean with the other powers because they assumed their naval supremacy would be permanent.

But the Peace of Paris produced its own problems. The French had little hope of regaining their position in Canada, and so any subsequent effort would have to be made in the Caribbean. Choiseul, the dynamic French minister, himself with West Indian connections, clearly regarded the period after 1763 only as a pause before finding a suitable opportunity for revenge. The lesson of the importance of seapower had been learnt, and France was determined to fight a Caribbean war without a European entanglement.

In the period following the peace of Paris, the French sugar colonies began a tremendous boom in production that lasted until the French Revolution. What Dr Eric Williams called 'the most amazing phenomenon in colonial development' was due to closer supervision, more skilful cultivation, better canes and the much greater extent of virgin land available on the French islands (3). St Domingue is much larger than Jamaica; Martinique and Guadeloupe than the British islands in the Leeward and Windward groups. British planters also increased production, but at a much slower rate, and only by an extravagant use of labour, manuring and new canes. They watched the French progress despondently, blaming it on the influx of slaves during the Seven Years War, and they accused the American colonists of making French sugar production feasible at all.

As American population and production had steadily increased, an indigenous American capitalism had grown up, based largely on shipping and distilling. The British sugar colonies proved inadequate as producers of raw materials for American industry, so the Americans quite simply turned to the French and the Spanish colonies for supplies. Lumber and provisions were sold to the French, either directly or through the 'free ports' of St Eustatius or Monte Cristi on Santo Domingo. Other Americans extended their triangular slaving voyages to a sort of quadrilateral, by selling their slaves in British colonies and buying molasses from the French colonies at almost give-away prices (**28**).

This trade had continued all through the Seven Years War. In 1757 the Commander-in-Chief Lord Loudoun had written to Chatham, calling the American traders 'a lawless set of smugglers who continually supply the Enemy with What Provisions they want and bring back their goods in Barter for them'. Three years later, the Governor of Pennsylvania believed 'a very great part of the principal merchants of this City (Philadelphia) engaged in a trade with the French Islands in the West Indies'. It was clear that new legislation would have to be passed to make the protectionist system work. The Molasses Act of 1733, theoretically rigorous, had never been enforced.

The new legislation, introduced by Grenville in 1764, was the Sugar Act, more correctly called the Plantations Act. This reduced the duty to be paid by Americans on foreign molasses from 6d per gallon, which the Americans rather too indignantly claimed to be prohibitive, to 3d, and this was to be collected by a more efficient customs system and more alert naval patrols. Originally the new duty was to have been fixed at 2d per gallon, but this was raised in response to a characteristic display of West Indian pressure.

It should not be thought that the Sugar Act was introduced primarily for the benefit of the sugar colonies. It was, in the words of Professor Harlow, 'a comprehensive and constructive attempt to remould the economy of the British imperial state'. There was much more to it than just protection of British sugar producers. By banning rum exports from the West Indies, the Act gave the Americans a monopoly in distilling. Its main new feature, however, was to provide revenue, and not simply to control trade, and it was this that led to constitutional objections (**44**).

Increased revenue had been made necessary by the rapidly increasing costs of colonial defence. During the Seven Years War, 10,000 regular troops had been kept in North America, plus a large fleet. American defence was costing £200,000 p.a., and West Indian about £100,000. In view of these estimated costs, the expected yield of £45,000 from the duty on molasses and the later £60,000 p.a. from the Stamp Act do not seem excessive. The former at least would presumably be passed on to the French planters, and there was a comfortable margin between wholesale and retail rum prices in the American colonies.

The final proof that the Sugar Act was not a surrender to West Indian pressure is that only two years later the British government reduced the duties on raw sugars and on molasses to 1*d* per gallon. In addition, a 'free port' in Dominica was opened to legalise some American smuggling and to open Spanish ports to British manufacturers.

This book does not offer a general discussion of the causes of the American War of Independence, but it is interesting to enquire why the American and the British West Indian colonists aligned on different sides. There were many close personal links between the two groups of colonists, and economically they had been complementary. Many settlers of the Carolinas had originally come from Barbados and other 'saturated' islands, and it was natural for many of the loyalists who left the mainland colonies after the war to migrate to the West Indies. There was an attempt by the Continental Congress to attract representatives from the West Indies, but in the event delegates only came from New Providence in the Bahamas.

The Stamp Act also applied to the West Indian colonies, and there was some rioting in the islands, especially in St Kitts and Nevis, although this may have been due to the leadership of American sailors in harbour. The Houses of Assembly in Jamaica in 1775 and Barbados in 1776 sent petitions to England asking for understanding for the Americans. These petitions were probably more sincere than those of British industrial and commercial towns, which Horace Walpole claimed were motivated by the colonists' refusal to pay any debts until the Act was repealed.

In spite of this basic sympathy, the two groups of colonists were on opposing sides in the final analysis. Up to the last, the West Indians did their utmost to avert a war, but ultimately they had no choice. They depended on Britain buying almost all their crop; they relied exclusively on the navy for protection; they had failed to develop either a diversified economy or an indigenous capitalist system. Their great landowners were absentee in England, depriving the remaining colonists of natural leadership.

It should be noted that the plantation colonies of North America had turned increasingly against the slave trade, because over-production had depressed tobacco prices. Jefferson tried to indict Britain as the organiser of the trade in the Declaration of Independence, and the colonies banned the trade—but not slavery itself—during and after the Revolution: Delaware in 1776, Virginia in 1778, Maryland in 1783, the Carolinas in 1787 and 1794 and Georgia in 1798 (**45, 46**).

THE WAR

The War of American Independence affected the plantation colonies in two ways. First, the plantation colonies of North America seceded from the empire as part of the United States. As such they were excluded from the trade system of Great Britain for a while after 1783, and this harmed their economy as well as the tobacco interests in England and Scotland. It shattered the old economy of Glasgow, ruined Whitehaven, and depressed Bristol.

Secondly, the sugar colonies were the scene of the usual sharp fighting. France in 1778 and Spain in 1779 came into the war on the American side, sensing a golden opportunity to curb British imperial expansion. In 1780 the Dutch also came into the war against Great Britain, largely as the result of incidents over the right of search at sea, and so the three largest continental naval powers were aligned against Great Britain, at a time when the latter was increasingly involved in a military struggle in North America (**47**).

The French sent troops to help the Americans, and their fleet played a vital part in the war at Yorktown, being repaired and provisioned for the first time in the western hemisphere. This French effort was mainly in the Caribbean, and to counter this threat British troops were withdrawn from Rhode Island and Philadelphia.

The heavy commitments of the British forces, coupled with the superiority of the Combined Fleet, working seasonally in the northern and southern theatres, meant that France had an almost unbroken run of successes between 1778 and 1782. In 1778 the French captured Dominica, a gain temporarily offset by the loss of St Lucia to a British force. In the next year St Vincent and Grenada were taken by the French, and after Yorktown the victorious

French admiral, de Grasse, captured St Kitts, Nevis and Montserrat'. Contrary winds held him off Barbados, and only a sensational naval victory, won by Rodney in the Saintes passage in 1782, saved Jamaica from invasion and probable occupation.

Once again, the colonial balance had been dictated by seapower. The British, however, did not go completely empty-handed. They battened on the Dutch colonies, which had been immune in previous conflicts as the mother country steered a careful course of neutrality between England and France. The most spectacular achievement was the capture of St Eustatius by the opportunist Rodney in 1781, when Holland had only just entered the war, and the colonists of the 'free port' were still not aware of the fact. Rodney captured between 150 and 250 ships of all nationalities and stores worth some £3 million. Dazzled by his prize, Rodney remained so long in St Eustatius that de Grasse was able to capture island after island, and also gain local command of the sea in the northern theatre. Other Dutch colonies on the mainland of South America, Berbice, Essequibo and Demerara, surrendered to an expedition from Barbados, while Saba, St Martin and the unsavoury Surinam were also occupied.

THE TREATY OF VERSAILLES

The crushing victory of the Saintes not only saved Jamaica, but also restored British bargaining power at the peace negotiations. The major element in the treaty was, of course, the independence of the American colonies, which both shattered the structure of the Atlantic plantation economy, and also presented alarming new problems to the defenders of Protection. In the Caribbean itself the only change was that Tobago was ceded to France. All other colonies, including the Dutch, were returned to their former owners. The subsequent rapid development of Tobago as a sugar colony indicates again the non-expansionist attitude of the British planters and the enterprise of the French in this period.

The loss of the American colonies could have meant that the sugar islands once more might have become the pampered favourites of the empire. But this did not happen. The day of the monopoly producer and the closed market was coming to an end. The rapidly growing industrial interests in Britain were ever less concerned with the islands as markets. They turned their attention to the United States, South America and, particularly, the East. In all these areas there were raw materials and huge potential markets (**table 3,** p. 142). Shelburne in 1782 could say that the British preferred trade to dominion. The expense of defending colonies in the incessant wars and of buying their artificially expensive products could be avoided.

But this fundamental shift did not happen at once, or entirely because of the loss of the American colonies (**52**). For a while the government attempted to shore up the remains of the imperial system, and this left America, now independent, outside it. Americans were not allowed to trade with the British sugar colonies, which protested loudly at this threat to their survival, since they were dependent on American supplies, but their demands were ignored once again. The government was more concerned about the danger of the British mercantile marine being overwhelmed by American rivalry. The old theme of naval security—dominant in much of the thinking behind the slave trade and protection—asserted itself once again.

Certain trade from America was allowed. Virginian tobacco was given preference over Spanish in Britain until 1826—but the total share of American exports to Britain and the British West Indies fell from 79 per cent before the Revolution to only 47 per cent after it.

From 1784 a new Committee of the Privy Council for Trade began a full-scale enquiry into Anglo-American trade, upon the pretext of a West Indian petition. Its report, largely reflecting Jenkinson's ideas, fixed British trade policy until 1794. Having excluded Americans from legitimate trade with the British sugar colonies, Jenkinson attempted to substitute Irish and Canadian foodstuffs for American, and to develop British trade with the Spanish empire by extending the 'free port' system, from which the Americans were also excluded. New food plants suitable for the West Indies were sought all over the world—Bligh and the *Bounty* were on such a mission seeking breadfruit plants—and cotton-growing experiments were encouraged in the British West Indies and West Africa. All this energy and experimentation were nevertheless fundamentally conservative. Jenkinson himself was concerned with preserving the fabric of the old imperial system (**53**).

The exclusion of American traders from the British sugar islands had three major consequences. First, and to the British planters most important and disastrous, the costs of all provisions soared. Barrel-stave prices quadrupled; rice, meat and fish more than doubled. When the severe hurricanes of 1784–86 devastated the now vital provision grounds, the Lieutenant-Governor of Jamaica reported 15,000 slaves had died of starvation. France saw the chance of 'adopting' the British ex-colonies and becoming the European terminus of American trade, without having to shoulder the burden of running an empire.

The Americans now concentrated on trade with the booming French colonies. Slaves and supplies were poured in, and the products were taken to maintain American distilleries and refineries. The French, Spanish and Dutch 'free ports' were open to the Americans, and, as a result, interest in the British 'free ports' declined (**32**).

Lastly, smuggling in the Caribbean became rife. The planters had little real alternative, and the Americans in their fast vessels were prepared to take the risk to exploit the price boom. The Royal Navy was employed in stopping the smuggling, and with the lure of better prize money, the fleet incurred immense unpopularity for its energy.

The British sugar colonies, virtually the sole relic of the old empire, underwent a period of crisis. No longer favoured by public opinion or government at home, and now rivalled by the French colonies, the planters found costs soaring, profits dwindling. The better planters tried new methods and attempted to diversify: most economised, often at the expense of the slaves and efficiency: the worst ran up bigger mortgages and larger debts. The process of selling out began. Disaster was only avoided briefly by the effects of the French Revolution in the Caribbean and the long period of war from 1792, which ruined the French colonies and gave a breathing-space to the British planters.

A last effect of the American Revolution should be noticed. Clarkson, a pioneer of the abolition of the slave trade, perceived that the loss of the American colonies helped his cause. The removal of the American slave plantations and the rapid decline of the West Indian ones had made abolition of the slave trade a possibility.

11 The French Revolution

The decade after 1783 saw the French West Indies at the peak of their prosperity. They had defeated their British rivals in the struggle for the markets of Europe, they enjoyed open trade with the United States, and they benefited from the friendly trade relations between the two mother countries that lasted until the Revolution.

The colony that typified this French achievement was St Domingue, the western half of the old Spanish colony of Hispaniola. The French had moved into this virtually unpopulated area in the late seventeenth century, and in the three decades before the Revolution the planters exploited a slave economy to produce enormous quantities of sugar from fertile land. In 1789 there were 32,000 whites and 450,000 negro slaves in the colony; 700 French ships plied between France and the colony, employing some 80,000 men. St Domingue and its re-exported products accounted for two-thirds of France's foreign commerce. This one colony by itself equalled the production of the whole British West Indies, and comfortably undersold it (**41**).

Apart from the older and still prosperous islands of Martinique and Guadeloupe, the French could point to another striking example of colonial enterprise. The Spanish colony of Trinidad had never been properly developed, and so in 1783, as a result of French initiative, Spain issued a *cedula* or decree allowing French immigration on very favourable terms. In the next fourteen years the colony boomed. The white population grew from 126 to 2,400, the free coloured from 245 to 4,900, and the negro slaves from 310 to a sensational 10,000. There were 468 plantations and 159 sugar mills. Again the large amount of virgin soil enabled the planters of Trinidad to out-produce and undersell the exhausted British colonies (**34**).

But, however successful the French planters in the Caribbean were at this time, they were still operating a slave system. The huge disparity of numbers and the hardships of slave life as always created an explosive situation. 'A slave colony is a town under siege; one lives on barrels of gunpowder', wrote a governor of St Domingue. This situation applied to both French and English colonies, and, to a markedly lesser degree, to Spanish. Fear of slave risings was a constant conditioning factor in the thinking of West Indians, and regular outbreaks of slave violence from the earliest days of the system gave them good cause.

The French Revolution, with its explicit doctrines of Liberty and Equality, was bound to have serious repercussions on the plantation colonies, since the relationships of colony to mother country and of slave to master had to be re-examined [**doc. 30**]. In the radical climate of thought before the Revolution both these relationships had already been discussed, and the trend was towards greater freedom in both respects. Turgot, Louis XV's great finance minister, advocated in place of protection 'complete freedom of trade, charging them only the cost of their defence and administration'. In France before the Revolution there was an active organisation for the emancipation of the slaves, known as *Les Amis des Noirs*, which was supported by the king, part of the court and some sections of the bourgeoisie. They remained active during the Revolution, and were largely responsible for keeping the interests of the slave and the free coloured before the Assemblies (**4**).

When the Estates-General was called in 1789, the colonies sent representatives, armed with the usual *cahiers des doléances*. Some of these representatives were accepted, and remained when the National Assembly was formed, but it must be remembered that both the delegates and the grievances came from the planter class, which hoped for colonial autonomy, leaving political power in the hands of the *grands blancs*—(the planters)—with slavery maintained.

That they failed to achieve these aims was due to the liberal elements in the Assembly. In spite of the planter representatives the National Assembly gave the franchise and full civil rights to the free coloured population of St Domingue. This created a complicated situation, since the 'free coloureds' were almost as numerous as the whites due to the French system of manumission, and in many cases were more prosperous than the poorer whites in the colony.

The planter oligarchy in the colony refused to accept the National Assembly's decrees, with the result that the 'free coloureds' rose in arms when they heard the news from France [**doc. 31**]. With the two dominant minority groups of the colony at one another's throats, the Negro slaves saw their moment to rise. In August 1791 a savage slave revolt swept across the northern plains. The 'free coloureds' tried to encourage the slaves against the whites, a disastrous policy that resulted in their own elimination. The Negroes and the whites were left, with the English and the Spanish sending help to their fellow-planters (**41, 42**).

From this turmoil the astonishing Negro leader, Toussaint l'Ouverture, emerged to become dictator of the French colony, taking over the Spanish half of the island, Santo Domingo, recreating the economy without using slavery, and establishing relationships with both Britain and the United States.

In 1792 slavery in the French empire had been abolished by the Assembly, partly in the hope of rallying negro support, and this move was confirmed by the Jacobins in 1794, when the colonies were given full provincial status as well. The principles of the Revolution had been carried out at the expense of imperial power.

This was a price that Napoleon Bonaparte was not prepared to pay. He set out to reverse some of the more doctrinaire actions of the Revolution, and to restore certain aspects of the *ancien régime* that he thought desirable. To this end Napoleon set about rebuilding a French empire in the New World. Louisiana was reacquired from Spain, and his brother-in-law, General Leclerc, was sent with 20,000 men to restore order in St Domingue. Toussaint was tricked, captured and dispatched to France before the French army fell victim to fever. Slavery was unwisely re-established in Guadeloupe, causing justifiable alarm amongst the freed slaves of St Domingue; just how justified was shown by Leclerc's secret orders to do this in St Domingue also when the time was ripe [**doc. 32**].

But Napoleon's colonial ambitions were not those closest to his heart. With the renewal of the war against England in 1803, and faced by the apparently insoluble problem of St Domingue, Napoleon cut his losses by ordering his troops in the island to surrender in Jamaica, while arranging to sell Louisiana to the United States, a move calculated to strengthen sympathy between the two countries.

St Domingue, left to itself, experienced an amazing series of Negro rulers. Dessalines became emperor of Haiti, but under his successor, Christophe, the island virtually ceased to produce sugar.

Thus the greatest rival to the British sugar colonies, by staging the only successful colonial revolt in the Caribbean, was eliminated.

THE BRITISH WEST INDIES
AND THE FRENCH REVOLUTION

The reactions of the British planter class to the slave revolutions of St Domingue were entirely predictable. Their first concern was to prevent any similar troubles in their own colonies, and for this reason the policy of rarely arming Negroes remained in force, even though the few that were armed seem to have been, with odd exceptions, loyal.

The major problem in this respect in the British colonies involved the famous Maroons of Jamaica. This people of runaway slaves lived in the inaccessible mountains of Jamaica and had been tolerated since their last rising in 1734. In 1795 they took advantage of the confusion and rose again. It is possible that they were stirred up by French agents, but in any case they terrified Jamaican planters who envisaged a mass slave rising. A regiment had to be recalled from St Domingue to crush the rising. The Maroon activists were deported to Nova Scotia, of all places, and suffered there until humanitarians in England arranged for them to be moved again to Sierra Leone (59).

Having put their own house in order as best they could, the British planters attempted to deal with the problem of St Domingue. As soon as war broke out between the two countries in 1792—once again certainly not for Caribbean reasons—the English seized the opportunity of attacking St Domingue, not only as the great sugar rival, but as the hotbed of slave disorder.

Pitt, the son of the minister who had used the Caribbean to such advantage in the Seven Years War, appears to have been dazzled by the prospect of West Indian pickings. Although he himself had been impressed by Wilberforce's campaign against the slave trade and publicly professed to be a pupil of Adam Smith, Pitt planned to emulate his father's war tactics, without giving any sign that he understood the wider strategy. Dr Eric Williams goes so far as to say that Pitt dropped his support of the abolitionists because he believed that he could capture St Domingue, but that he could only make it productive if slaves were available for its exploitation (3). This is certainly arguable, in the light of statements by Pitt that St Domingue was a 'noble compensation' for the loss of America and 'a glorious addition to the dominion, navigation, trade and manufactures of Britain', but there are other more valid political and psychological reasons for Pitt turning away from reforms in general, of which abolition of the slave trade is only one example.

Until Pitt's death, the major British military effort was in the Caribbean, and the French were only able to retaliate by naval raids such as those by Missiessy and Villeneuve in 1805. In the meanwhile French forces dominated Europe, and Napoleon had closed most of the ports of Europe to British trade by the Berlin Decrees, so that the British sugar colonies were in the ironic position of having regained a European monopoly without being able to take advantage of it. For this very limited gain Pitt sacrificed up to 80,000 men in the various Caribbean campaigns, losses as severe as those suffered in the much more effective Peninsular War.

The war in the West Indies followed the usual pattern when Britain held command of the sea. In 1793–4 Martinique, Tobago, St Lucia and Guadeloupe were all captured, although the French showed local resilience by recapturing the last two, and countered further by inciting the Caribs in Dominica and the Maroons in Jamaica against the British. In 1796 Abercrombie carried out a successful campaign to capture St Lucia once again, to take Demerara and, in the following year, Trinidad, which surrendered without a shot being fired. Against this run of minor successes must be set the total failure of the expedition to St Domingue.

The softness of the Treaty of Amiens in 1802 emphasised the essential irrelevance of Pitt's Caribbean strategy since the terms included the return of all conquests during the war with the exception of Trinidad, which had been Spanish.

But this odd peace was shortlived. When war broke out again in 1803, the whole process of reconquering the islands was repeated. At the Treaty of Vienna in 1814–15 there were rather wider changes of ownership. Britain for strategic reasons took St Lucia and Tobago, and kept Trinidad, partly as an entrepôt for illegal trade to South America. The Dutch Guiana colonies were purchased, and their enormous development followed immediately. Demerara sugar was introduced into the British household.

The real significance of the treaty in imperial terms, however, lies in the fact that the Caribbean acquisitions were regarded as of only minor importance. The transfer to Britain of the Cape of Good

Hope, Mauritius and Ceylon was greeted much more enthusiastically, as securing for the mother country a major share in eastern trade. Even the guarantee that Antwerp and Flushing would stay out of French hands, implied in the creation of a strong Netherlands state in the treaty, was seen as being worth 'twenty Martiniques'. This, the last in a long series of treaties, clearly marked the decline in prestige of the plantation empire.

THE EFFECTS OF THE REVOLUTION

One incidental effect of the French Revolution on the West Indies was the setback it inflicted on both the abolition of the slave trade and emancipation of slaves. Pitt, as we have seen, dropped the abolitionist cause, delaying passage of an Act of Parliament until 1807. The slave explosion on St Domingue was a terrible warning—in West Indian eyes at least—of the dangers of any reform. In France, as in England, emancipation was seen as a revolutionary or Jacobin measure, and so reactionary governments from 1802 onwards turned away from it, and France was later than Britain in finally abolishing slavery.

The fundamental upheavals in St Domingue meant that the colony never recovered its productive capacity. Dessalines and Christophe did not follow Toussaint's attempt to reintroduce a plantation economy without slavery, along the lines of a 'kibbutz', and they encouraged a typical peasant economy. This meant that sugar virtually ceased to be grown or manufactured, and that coffee became the island's main crop as early as 1810. These figures illustrate this dual process (41):

	Sugar (lb)	*Coffee* (lb)
1791	163,405,220	68,151,180
1802	53,400,000	34,370,000
1804	47,600,000	31,000,000
1818	1,896,000	20,280,300
1825	2,020	36,034,300

The other newly important French-sponsored sugar producing colony, Trinidad, was also no longer producing. After its annexation by Britain there was no immediate plantation development, not as a concession to the hard-pressed West Indian interests, but solely because such a development would require a massive influx of slaves at a time when abolition of the trade was a live issue in Parliament. Canning could say in the House of Commons in 1802: 'If there was a question of suddenly cultivating such as Island as Trinidad, we must make up our minds to the destruction of about a million of the human species' (**34**).

With St Domingue and Trinidad out of commission, the recovery of British West Indian sugar might seem a real possibility. The first results of the war and the St Domingue upheaval were encouraging price rises for sugar on the London market. In 1792 the London price was 54s 3d–56s 6d per cwt. This rose to 69s 2d by 1796, where it stayed approximately until the peace of Amiens when prices slumped to 35s 6d in 1802. To the undisguised relief of the planters war began again and prices recovered to about 60s until the effect of the Berlin Decrees and a glut of sugar on the London market, now also being provided by captured sugar colonies, caused a sharp slump after 1807. At this point freight charges and insurance premiums, both increased as a result of the war, along with the various duties were not covered by the price. The West Indians enjoyed one more little boom when sugar prices soared to 100s in 1814, as a result partly of the 1812–14 war with the United States and partly of the liberation of eastern Europe and its reopening as a market.

But from 1814 the trend was clearly downwards: 73s 4d by the end of 1814, 41s 4d in 1819, 30s by 1828, 28s 7d by 1829 and a disastrous 23s 8d in 1831. These were the years when disaster finally overtook the debt-laden plantation system. In Professor Pares's words: 'The sugar market was ruled by the economic and financial rhythm of the country in general' (**30**).

The Revolutionary and Napoleonic wars introduced another element which contributed to this decline. Rival sugar producers appeared. St Domingue had collapsed, but it could be replaced. The conquest by Britain of the Dutch Guiana colonies of Berbice, Demerara and Essequibo in 1796 was the signal for a dramatic expansion there. In four years cotton production rose from 2,425 bales to 31,433: sugar from 1,483 hogsheads to 10,361: coffee from 1,937,230 lb. to 11,633,136 lb. Even after the abolition of the slave trade and emancipation this development continued with other forms of cheap labour imported from the East. Mauritius, acquired in 1814, soon became a major sugar producer, thriving on its easy access to the labour supply of India. Early in the nineteenth century, Cuba saw the chance to copy St Domingue, and later Brazil's huge plantations ensured the permanent decline of the British sugar colonies. As if this was not competition enough, the French and the Germans had been forced by the British naval blockade during the war to experiment with the production of sugar from beet, and this was to become available as an alternative.

The French Revolution broke up the French Caribbean empire, and it presented an ideological challenge to all slave systems. The subsequent wars seemed to offer a reprieve to British planters, but the gains made by Britain during the war were eventually to make the West Indies completely dispensable, since they no longer produced the bulk of Europe's sugar.

12 The Industrial Revolution

Dr Eric Williams states one of his conclusions to his book *Capitalism and Slavery* in these terms: 'The political and moral ideas of the age are to be examined in the very closest relation to the economic development' (3). In this context the obvious economic development of the century after 1750 is the sensational growth of British commerce and industry. This technological development seemingly had only a tenuous connection with the colonies. Dean Tucker stressed this point when he listed improvements in communications, changes in agriculture, technical inventions, lowered tariffs and more capital and concluded: 'All these things co-operating together would render any Country rich and flourishing, whether it had colonies or not.'

Dr Williams has put forward an alternative thesis which argues that the colonies were important in providing the stimulus for the 'take-off' for the Industrial Revolution, but that by the 1780s the colonial system was a hindrance to further growth, and as a result the industrialists lent their support to the attack on slavery and later on all preferential duties (3).

Much of this argument is convincing. Cotton was the outstanding growth industry in this period, and in this respect the colonies of the New World were significant as markets and as sources of raw material. By the 1770s cotton exports exceeded £300,000, and five sixths of these were to Africa or the plantations. However the really dramatic increase in cotton exports came between 1785, when they were just over £4 million, and 1830, when they exceeded £32 million, and the share to the plantation colonies was minor [**tables 2, 3**].

The production of raw cotton for the mills of Lancashire was an important contribution of the plantation colonies. In 1764 imports stood at around the £4 million level, 50 per cent coming from the British West Indies. By 1780 the islands sent 65 per cent of the total imports of £6½ million. By 1790 the British islands reached a peak with 70 per cent of the imports, and many plantations were beginning to diversify. But for the majority this chance came too late, as the British plantations lost their supremacy during the 1790s. By 1803 the United States was sending 45,000 bales of cheaper, low quality cotton to Britain, closely challenging the 57,000 bales from the British West Indies. From the turn of the century, the share of the British West Indies fell sharply, until it was only 7 per cent by 1820, and a mere 2¼ per cent in 1830 when the United States had won control of the Lancashire market with 75 per cent of the imports, while Brazil and the East Indies had surpassed the West Indies. The combination of the cotton gin, developed in 1792–3, and the continuation of slavery on the vast growing areas of the southern United States destroyed the West Indies as a competitor. But in any event the limited area of the British plantation colonies would have prevented them meeting the demands of the mature cotton industry [**table 1**].

The growth of markets, both inside and outside the British Isles made the Industrial Revolution possible, and it was natural for manufacturers to want to be in a position to sell to as many countries as possible and to buy raw material from the cheapest source. North American trade with Britain boomed after 1783, exposing the limitations of protectionism. South America became a prized market, and it was deliberate policy for Britain to help the Spanish colonies win their independence [**table 4**]. Canning wrote with satisfaction in 1824: 'The nail is driven. Spanish America is free and if we do not mismanage our affairs sadly she is English.'

The Far East was another growing market. In the decade after 1822 China and the East Indies increased their share of British exports from one twelfth to one tenth, while in the same ten years the share of the British West Indies fell from one ninth to one seventeenth, and this in a period when British exports rose by 50 per cent. This feature was not lost on contemporary observers. Cobden claimed that the only function of the West Indian colonies was 'to complicate and magnify our government expenditure, without improving our balance of trade'.

Nor could the colonies provide cheap food. Their sugar was not competitive with that of St Domingue up to 1792; nor with that of Mauritius, Brazil or Cuba in the nineteenth century. Refiners and distillers demanded cheaper supplies, and the attack on food tariffs, at its most spectacular over the Corn Laws, was equally concerned with sugar. The Anti-Corn Law League, it was claimed, was 'established on the same righteous principle as the Anti-Slavery Society'.

The most disputed point in Dr Williams's case concerns capital. He suggests that the colonial system provided much of the early capital for the Industrial Revolution. On the other hand, Professor Pares showed at great length that the planters were almost always in debt, and increasingly so. He concluded: 'Since colonies absorbed as much capital as they could get, they cannot have done much to build up capital in England, and thereby promote the Industrial Revolution.' Nor did Professor Pares find that the merchants handling the plantation trades invested widely in industry. He wrote:

> Since the most lucrative and important branches of colonial trade were those in which the English merchants acted as factors for the planter and these men had to employ all their capital and all they could get from their bankers in financing the trade . . . it is beginning to be clear that it was the agricultural rather than the colonial wealth of England that was tapped for industrial development in the later eighteenth century.

His analysis of the Pinney fortune shows that in 1817 £200,000 of the firm's total £340,000 capital was tied up in mortgages (**30**).

Dr Williams cites examples of West Indian capital behind certain industrial developments, notably the Great Western Railway and the South Wales slate industry (**3**), but it would seem that a much greater proportion of colonial money transferred to Britain went to finance the ostentatious expenditure of the absentee proprietors and their political ambitions. Rather late in the day there may have been some transfer of capital from the plantations to the safer investment of industry and railways, but it must be doubtful if this was on any considerable scale, at a time when the Industrial Revolution was creating its own capital. Professor Pares found an example of a Pinney removing £26,000 from the firm in 1836, and 'he seems to have invested part of this money in a cotton manufactory' (**30**).

So, to conclude, while there clearly was some investment of capital originating from the colonies in the Industrial Revolution, it has not been demonstrated that this was a considerable contribution. The investors in the slave trade, in Liverpool until latterly often small operators, probably would not have sought any further field of investment for their profits. The colonies and the slave trade undoubtedly provided a significant part of the demand for the products of the first stages of industrial expansion. In this same period the colonies made an effort to provide the necessary raw cotton, but quickly found this task beyond them.

By the time the British industrial classes found themselves able to take a part in politics, there were no remaining bonds between them and the colonies, which had proved inadequate as markets, and as suppliers of raw materials or food. They were unlikely to exert themselves in the defence of such colonies.

13 New Thinking

During the eighteenth century there occurred a major intellectual revolution, which affected philosophy, politics and economics. At the same time, there began a cultural movement that was to develop in the nineteenth century into Romanticism. Finally, the growth of humanitarian thinking, resulting from the concentration of social evils and the revival of middle-class nonconformity and evangelicalism, created the atmosphere for a series of great social reforms.

These three movements were basically independent, although there are frequent links and a resulting degree of cross-fertilisation. It is outside the scope of this book to examine the origins and development of these themes, but since they all implicitly or explicitly criticised and reassessed the colonial system as it existed, and particularly the key institution of slavery, the foundation of the plantation system, it is necessary to examine their effect in this field.

Political philosophers and economists launched shattering attacks on the two basic relationships of the imperial system—that between mother country and colony, and that between master and slave. These attacks were developed both on the continent and in Great Britain, but they were consciously and intimately linked. Locke's influence on the Philosophes is clear; he and Montesquieu were both antislavery. Dean Tucker taught Condorcet and the Physiocrats: Condorcet was president of the French abolitionist society, *Les Amis des Noirs*, rallying support with his great *Réflections sur l'esclavage des nègres* (1781). Rousseau opened Tom Paine's eyes, and the latter in turn inspired revolutionaries in France with his *Rights of Man*.

The philosophers based their thinking on the concept of common humanity, and this was easily developed into the cult of 'the noble savage'. Rousseau's superb opening to his *Contrat Social*—'Man is born free, but everywhere is in chains'—is the premise of his own political theory, but could obviously be applied directly to the vast number of men and women often actually in chains, the slaves. Tom Paine's *Rights of Man* was a deliberately provocative appeal for the unprivileged and unfranchised, but his Man was not specifically white or civilised or literate; he was only human. This challenge, and others like it, forced pro-slavery writers to base their defence of the institution on theories that negroes were in some way less than full human beings, and such writers found support in the writings of men as eminent as Thomas Jefferson and David Hume [**doc. 16**].

More directly political was the influence of Edmund Burke, who was close to the centre of eighteenth century British politics. In his brilliant attacks on government policy in India and America, he brought into question the right of one country to hold another subject, even as a colony, and also introduced the tenet that subject peoples had rights. The former point was not immediately applicable to the sugar colonies, which needed protection in both senses of the word, but the thesis could be refurbished when an articulate political group wanted to be rid of the encumbrance of the colonies. While Burke did not see slaves specifically as subject people in a political sense, he was critical of European treatment of slaves in his *European Government in America*.

The economists are even more important than the philosophers. Philosophical theories can be accepted or not, but economic facts of life are much more likely to change political opinion. Adam Smith, the Scots economist, was the most celebrated exponent of anti-colonial ideas. In his great work, *The Wealth of Nations*, published in 1776, he questioned the whole basis of the colonial system. He believed protection impeded the real development of the wealth of the country: he costed the colonies and found the balance heavily in debit: he argued that money wasted on the colonies could be much more profitably invested in industry, agriculture and commerce [**doc. 29**]. It is significant that Smith's 1759 *Theory of Moral Sentiments*, criticising the planters' way of life, made much less impact than his economic attack.

In *The Wealth of Nations*, book v, chapter 3, Adam Smith summed up: 'The rulers of Great Britain have, for more than a century past, amused the people with the imagination that they possessed a great empire on the west side of the Atlantic. This empire, however, had existed in the imagination only.' His teachings seemed to receive irrefutable support from the great increase of trade between Britain and the newly independent United States after 1783.

However, his ideas were slow to become political policy. Pitt may have told Smith in 1787, 'We are all your scholars', but he nevertheless still spent men and money in the Revolutionary Wars in trying to extend the plantation empire. It is easy to find leading nineteenth century statesman still following a policy somewhere between Smith and the discredited Protectionism (**60**).

Dean Josiah Tucker, writing at the same time as Adam Smith, singled out the economics of the colonial system of the eighteenth century for particular scorn. He questioned the value of the colonies in terms of both quantity and quality of life. He concluded scathingly: 'It is not the Mother Country which meddles with the Colonies, but the Colonies which meddle with the Mother Country.' Tucker, although less celebrated than Adam Smith in England, was particularly influential in France, where the Physiocrats, who were constructing a whole corpus of theory to criticise existing institutions of all kinds, modelled their colonial ideas on Tucker's writings. From France these ideas were taken up by the liberal intellectuals of Spain and Portugal, so that almost every colonial power found that acceptance of empire as a self-evident advantage was no longer tenable.

These economic theories were to be put into practice politically as Free Trade. Pitt, Canning and Huskisson gradually incorporated the theory into practical government action, and the work of Huskisson and Peel, both Tories, was to mark the abandonment of the plantation empire. Huskisson in 1825 examined the great growth of trade with the United States, and asked the difficult questions: 'Whether their emancipation from the commercial thraldom of the colonial system has really been prejudicial to the trade and industry of Great Britain? Is there no useful admonition to be derived from this example?' The answers were all too clear to the merchants and manufacturers of industrial Britain (**76, 77**).

This anti-imperialism, in terms of its uselessness, was pursued further by the Utilitarians and radicals. Bentham himself wrote a pamphlet, *Emancipate your Colonies*, for the 1793 French Convention. This unique blend of philosophy and political action brought the issues into the main stream of English political debate [**doc. 34**]. Thus Empire was an issue during the struggles associated with the 1832 Reform Bill and the Corn Laws in the 1840s, and since the West Indian interest aligned with the conservatives against the liberal and radical groupings, they suffered when their causes were eventually lost. The colonial and slavery debates reflect vividly just one of the great splits in the British ruling class, almost to be described as the alienation of the intellectuals, which made possible the total revolution that took place in nineteenth century England and France.

In conditioning public opinion the artists and poets of the time also played their part. Here again it was Rousseau who stated the theme with his basic concept of unspoiled natural man—the noble savage. This was to be a theme in the Romantic movement, which, with its unbridled expression of passions and love of the exotic, found the subject of slavery exactly to its taste. Géricault, himself a liberal opponent of the restored monarchy in France, explored the theme in drawings, and this was to be further exploited by his admirer, Delacroix, who painted the slave trade in the same style as his 'Massacre at Chios,' showing the slaves in a dramatic and idealised group of beautiful negroes being shipped away from Africa, expressing noble emotions, such as grief, love of country, and stoic suffering.

In England the poets, rather than the painters, turned to the theme of slavery. A subject for one of Wordsworth's 'Poems dedicated to National Independence and Liberty', 1802, was Toussaint L'Ouverture, significantly referred to as 'miserable chieftain'. The poem ends stirringly:

> Thou hast left behind
> Powers that will work for thee; air, earth and skies;
> There's not a breathing of the common mind
> That will forget thee: thou hast great allies;
> Thy friends are exultations, agonies,
> And love, and man's unconquerable mind.

Cowper wrote 'The Negro's Complaint' as early as 1788, and it was distributed as propaganda by the Abolitionist Society. The poem rejects the whole basis of slavery, simply in terms of human rights. A passage from the poem runs:

> Still in thought as free as ever,
> What are England's rights, I ask,
> Me from my delights to sever,
> Me to torture, me to task?

Fleecy locks, and black complexion
Cannot forfeit nature's claim;
Skins may differ, but affection
Dwells in white and black the same.

This concept of basic humanity was taken to its spiritual conclusion in one of Blake's *Songs of Innocence* (1789), 'The Little Black Boy', where the poet uses a Negro child, not specifically a slave, to develop his stated belief that 'everything that lives is holy' [**doc. 33**]. Blake, as might be expected, completely rejected any rational defence of slavery in terms of emotion alone, and this was to be the technique of many abolitionists in the political field, when faced with commercial or naval arguments in favour of the slave trade.

The growth of an active religious morality must not be overlooked in the conditioning of public opinion. In Britain this was expressed in the growth of nonconformity and the emergence of an evangelical Anglicanism. These developments were vitally necessary, since the Church of England in the colonies had identified itself with the planters, Anglican Christianity being virtually a white prerogative. This was reflected by a wide acceptance of slavery within the Church in England, many churchmen being considerable slave-owners.

Nonconformists took an altogether more dynamic line. The Quakers had always been more decisively against slavery. Even though Friends had owned slaves in the early years of Pennsylvania, that colony had been the first to abolish slavery in 1727. In England the first committee to attack the problem on a national scale was Quaker. Wesley came out against slavery in his *Thoughts on Slavery* (1774), and Methodists attacked the institution at home and in the colonies, where they had become the leading missionary society by 1830 [**doc. 35**].

The new Christianity alerted the consciences of the middle classes. Slavery and Christian ethics can hardly be regarded as compatible. Indeed in some societies, including the plantation colonies, Christianity was regarded as revolutionary and seditious.

There is little evidence to suggest that this ardour was synthetic. Dr Eric Williams implies that religion was as good a stick to attack the planters with as any, and that a hypocritical campaign was launched to mask deeper economic motivation. The true picture must be more complex, and is probably nearer Professor Burn's summary: 'The dominant elements in any given society will seek the combination of what they want with what they believe that society needs' (2).

The doctrinal changes outlined in this chapter amounted to a revolution in themselves. All of them, for their different reasons, operated against the acceptance of slavery, the slave trade, and, by implication, the plantation empires. At the moment when this empire was at its least efficient, when it appeared to be an obstruction to new economic interests, philosophy, political theory, art, poetry and religious enthusiasm combined to undermine its foundations.

Part Three

CONCLUSION

14 Abolition of the Slave Trade

The movement that led to the abolition of the slave trade has been described in detail by generations of liberal historians. The name of the prime mover, Wilberforce, has almost unique fame amongst nineteenth century reformers. There has inevitably been a reaction to this approach, stated most clearly by Dr Eric Williams, who argues that the humanitarian attack was basically a cover for the economic-based motives of many of the movement's supporters (3).

The second section of this book has been an outline of the growing factors operating against the colonial system and against slavery towards the end of the nineteenth century. Although a depressed Horace Walpole wrote in 1781 of 'the moment of the fall of an Empire', it is important to understand that with a transition of this sort there is no clear turning-point. Thus neither the American, French nor the Industrial Revolutions by themselves created the sort of impact that made political opinion instantly turn against the old system. The most closely argued economic analyses, the most cogent political philosophy, the most moving paintings and poems in themselves cannot produce immediate change. Professor Harlow has argued that the founding of the second British empire dates from the loss of the American colonies, but he very rightly repeatedly stressed that this was a growth that ran parallel to the existence and even the continued development of the first plantation empire (52).

By the last two decades of the century the conditions for the assault on the old colonial system had been created. The wars fought to annex or defend the colonies had proved tremendously costly and not particularly rewarding. The old plantation system—or what was left of it—was showing itself to be increasingly inefficient: it has been well called 'a luxury defended by a monopoly'. It no longer served as a considerable market, as an important provider of cheap food or raw materials, nor was the capital the system produced any longer vital to economic expansion at home. The industrial and commercial classes had good cause for regarding the colonies as obstructions to 'natural' expansion, and it was these very people who finally emerged into central politics in Britain and France in the 1830s.

It was in this climate that the humanitarian movement was launched that was to secure the abolition of the slave trade and emancipation of the slaves themselves. Dr Williams himself calls these men the 'spearhead of the onslaught which destroyed the West Indian system and freed the Negro' (3).

The initiative for the movement came almost entirely from within European society. Very few voices were raised against the institution of slavery from the West Indies. Clearly this is not be wondered at in the case of the planters, but the planters were the ruling élite, and one looks in vain for any equivalent of a 'bourgeois' protest (37).

In England the movement was an interesting blend of religious zeal, popular protest, and hard political pressure. The Quakers' Abolitionist Committee was in existence when the wider movement got under way. Methodists and Evangelicals joined in, and the movement gained much strength from the fact that it achieved the status of a religion, so that its opponents were automatically some sort of heretics, or worse (56).

Religious zeal was not the only technique employed. There was also a shrewd practicality in the campaign. Granville Sharp fought a brilliant and ultimately successful legal battle which culminated in the 1772 Sommersett case, which freed 15,000 slaves in England, and implicitly posed the question of the legality of slavery as well as its morality. Clarkson, a founder member of the Society for the Abolition of the Slave Trade and later one of the Clapham Sect, assiduously collected evidence from any quarter, sometimes at danger to his person, to be presented to Parliament. As early as 1787 the tiny Colony of Sierra Leone was founded as a refuge for freed slaves (59). The public campaign, with its election addresses, Wedgwood plaques, and its massive propaganda was nothing if not practical. In 1792 an abolitionist Bill before Parliament was backed by 519 separate petitions.

Ultimately, any success for the Abolitionists had to be registered in Parliament, and it was there that Wilberforce did his best work. Again, he was not the pioneer, but he was influential and single-minded once his interest had been aroused, and the historian has to give him his due for the passage of the Act abolishing the Trade.

He was a complex personality, and has aroused both adulation and bitter hostility in his own time and amongst historians (**3, 56, 57**).

The story of the passage of the Bill is again well known. As early as 1776 Hartley had introduced a motion calling the trade 'contrary to the laws of God and the rights of man'. From 1788, encouraged by the active interest of Pitt, abolition was a live cause, with parliamentary committees hearing evidence, and in 1791 a full Privy Council enquiry was launched.

This apparently favourable atmosphere was spoilt by the increasing violence of the French Revolution, the outbreak of the war with France, and the dramatic events on St Domingue. All reform was tainted with revolution: reformers were seen as Jacobins. Lady Spencer was told: 'Your friend Mr Wilberforce will be very happy any morning to hand your Ladyship to the guillotine' (**6**). The war proved an impediment to the cause of abolition in France also, where it led to a fresh and much more cynical assessment of British motives for wanting to abolish the trade. Even Clarkson was regarded as a possible spy when he visited France to meet *Les Amis des Noirs*.

But abolition had too much impetus to be stopped permanently. As well as finding the general climate of opinion favourable at the turn of the century, there were other particular factors assisting the cause. Many of the better-established West Indian planters were in favour of the abolition of the slave trade itself. Their arguments were characteristic. They realised that the trade could supply slaves to the new British territories of Trinidad and Guiana to make them effective rivals of the older British colonies. They also felt that the British colonies were better stocked with slaves than the foreign West Indies, and that it would be in their interest if there was no further supply of slaves at all. Some of the more thoughtful planters seem to have realised that the abolition of the trade would disarm much of the feeling against the institution of slavery itself, since it was obvious that planters would have to take more care of the slaves if there was no hope of replacing them except by natural increase. This had for long been the attitude of Virginian slave-owners and some West Indians, like the planter-historian Bryan Edwards (**12**).

The careful accumulation of evidence about the shipping and seamen involved in the trade gave the abolitionists further valuable ammunition. They were able to refute the hoary myth that the slave trade was a nursery of seamen, by showing the horrifying death rate, the low standard of man employed, the age of the ships, and the bad conditions of service. Admirals ready to defend the trade could be found to the end, but the abolitionists—especially Clarkson and the ex-slaving captain Newton (**14**)—were able to persuade naval administrators of the first rank. Thus Lord Barham, a friend of Ramsay and Wilberforce, wrote of the trade: 'It destroys our seamen by the thousands, makes bankrupts of those employed in it, and is chiefly applied to the improvement of the French sugar colonies, which are the best nursery of their navy.'

Lastly, even the port of Liverpool was becoming less concerned about the trade, which had fallen into fewer hands, and some of these big firms had felt the pinch in the last years of the trade. Other forms of trade and the very profitable practice of wartime privateering meant that commercial interests no longer rallied so vociferously. Alderman Newnham, quoted in the abolitionist debate of May 1789 as an opponent of Wilberforce, sounds unconvincing: 'A proposition which, if carried, would fill the City with men suffering as much as the poor Africans . . . it would render the City of London one scene of bankruptcy and ruin' (E.H.D. XI).

Quite independent support for the abolitionists could be found in the writings of the travellers and missionaries who were beginning to penetrate into deeper Africa. Mungo Park in 1799 reported that slave hunters were devastating tribes in the hinterland, and that the trade run by Europeans on the coast was demoralising the whole continent (**15**) [**doc. 10**].

Pitt's support for the abolitionists in the early stages of the campaign had not been an unmixed blessing. Canning (E.H.D. XI) noticed that there was a strong body of opinion within Parliament in favour of the trade for no other reason than that Pitt opposed it, and since this was to be the equivalent of a free vote, it was able to show unaccustomed independence of Pitt in opposing it. Nevertheless Pitt's record on abolition is weak, and it was Fox and the Whigs who finally secured the passage of the Act in 1807.

What were the effects of the Act on the plantation empires? It certainly did not put an end to the trade. Even British ships continued illegally, and neither the death penalty nor the presence of naval squadrons on the coast were sufficient deterrents (**21**). Pressure was eventually brought onto other countries to follow the example of Great Britain, Denmark and the United States, but since France permitted the trade until 1819, Spain until 1820, and

Portugal officially until 1830, it seems certain that more slaves were carried across the Atlantic after abolition than before. The King of Bonney had a point when he remarked, on being told of the abolition: 'We tink trade no stop, for all we ju-ju men tell we so, for dem say you country no can niber pass God A'mighty.'

There was an increase in inter-colonial illegal slave trading, since the productivity of a slave in Trinidad or Guiana made him two or three times more valuable than he was in the older colonies (**34**).

It does appear that the conditions for slaves in the Caribbean did improve after abolition, both because of the difficulty of replacing them, and because planters feared emancipation as the next step. By 1824 the annual rate of wastage of slaves had fallen from the preabolition $2\frac{1}{4}$ per cent to $\frac{5}{8}$ per cent.

It has been questioned—by Dr Williams notably—whether the leaders in the abolitionist movement were originally concerned with emancipation. Clarkson's account of the struggle, published as early as 1808, gives a very clear analysis of the tactics involved, showing that abolition of the trade was a practical target, since it did not involve property, and that abolition and emancipation together might have proved too great a task (E.H.D. XI).

The total effect was to undermine the existing economy of the colonies. Possibly, under different economic conditions, abolition might have proved beneficial to the slave system, but one has to accept the well-informed Merivale's dictum: 'Slavery without the slave trade, and in the then circumstances of the colonies, was rather a loss than a gain.'

15 Emancipation of the Slaves

Between the abolition of the slave trade in the British empire and the emancipation of slaves there was a period of just over twenty-five years. This gap is a most interesting and surprising feature in the process which destroyed the plantation colonies.

The fervour of the abolitionists explains this delay to some extent. Clarkson and his committee deliberately decided to confine their efforts to abolishing the trade, and their very success had to some extent disarmed the movement. At that point many abolitionists dropped out of the second phase, either from a degree of fulfilment or exhaustion, or because they felt that abolition in itself would guarantee better conditions for the slaves. Others held that the disappearance of slavery would follow in due course, for economic reasons, and in the face of the new Christian morality they fondly hoped was sweeping the world. Thus it needed the shock of the arrest and subsequent death of the Rev. Smith after the 1823 Demerara slave riots to re-activate the movement. Clarkson had relinquished the leadership; Wilberforce, not a great reformer on most issues, did not become vitally interested in emancipation until about 1823; and the direction of the campaign was left in the timid hands of Buxton, the 'gradualist' *par excellence*. The name of the new society in 1823 emphasises this attitude: 'The Society for the Mitigation and Gradual Abolition of Slavery throughout the British Commonwealth.'

In the eyes of the abolitionists and of the planters, there was a very real difference between the slave trade and slavery itself. There was no obviously valid defence for the slave trade—although, of course, this did not prevent the defence of 'absolute necessity' being put forward—but in defence of slavery there was a whole range of arguments, from the persuasive to the feeble.

The strongest argument put forward in the colonies and in Parliament was that slaves were a form of property, sanctioned by colonial law and implicitly permitted by Parliament. The whole trend of eighteenth-century politics had been towards defence of property; so Englishmen managed to refer to Magna Carta to justify the slavery of non-Englishmen. Dr Johnson, as usual, had already exposed this paradox superbly: 'How is it that we hear the loudest yelps for liberty among the drivers of negroes?' [**doc. 14**]. But the appeal was effective in the unreformed British Parliament. A back-bencher argued: 'The property of the West Indies is at stake; and though men may be generous with their own property, they should not be so with the property of others'; Lord Wynford in 1832 talked of 'an end to all property' (**6**).

The planters had to base their defence of slavery on the concept of property because the total subordination of one person to another can only be explained in English law in terms of property. Once they had chosen this ground, they found they received the implied sanction of the Lockeian tradition. For this reason the Mansfield judgment in the Sommersett case, making slavery illegal in the British Isles, was a vital step in the long struggle against the slaveowners.

The House of Commons, dominated until the Reform Act by the landowning interest, was further influenced by other sentiments. It regarded national prestige in already old-fashioned terms of colonial strength, and saw a threat to slavery as a threat to the plantation empire without making an examination of that empire's true worth. In addition, they regarded with dread any suggestion that emancipation might weaken the country's naval strength, and this continued to be the cry of many eminent naval persons long after the abolition of the slave trade. This attitude was well expressed by Chief Justice Sheffield: 'We should find ourselves, like the Dutch, rich perhaps as individuals, but weak as a State.'

The planters also produced the alarming argument that any tampering with absolute slavery would lead to a repetition of the St Domingue atrocities. For a while this argument was accepted widely, but ultimately outbreaks of slave violence, such as the 1832 revolt in Jamaica, became the final argument for emancipation.

A rather different line was taken at the same time by planters and their allies, who claimed that slaves were being saved from a more barbarous existence, by being taken from Africa and being transported to the Caribbean where they, in theory, would come into contact with Christianity.

To support this argument, it was claimed that conditions on the plantations were not as brutal as painted by hostile propagandists, and planters took good care to impress visitors to this effect [**doc. 17**]. In pamphlets, verse [**doc. 15**] and cartoons (**23**), the lot of the negro was contrasted with that of the worker in English industrial cities, naturally, and not entirely without reason, to the latter's disadvantage (**36**).

The defenders of the institution were by no means exhausted. They argued with much 'evidence' from the Bible, from classical writers and from observation, that the Negroes were an inferior people, and therefore in some way intended for a subordinate role [**doc. 16**]. At all events they were certainly not to be regarded as 'full economic men', so that accepted rules of wages and production could not be applied to them.

Finally, and it has been mentioned that planters and abolitionists to some extent agreed, there was the wide belief that there was no need to legislate against slavery, since this would die a natural death. The Rev. G. W. Bridges, a Jamaican clergyman and not surprisingly Anglican, who was a firm advocate of the slave system, argued that slavery would collapse in the face of 'the new moral code which was to reform the earth and remodel the heart of man'. To some extent this fitted in with the political theory of conservatism stated fully by Burke that all valid reform has to be gradual, and that one cannot legislate for man 'like a piece of clockwork or a steam-engine'.

The movement against slavery had lost its impetus, as the leaders continued to fret about the remnants of the slave trade. The emancipators confined themselves to the belief that slavery was simply immoral in itself, and scarcely tackled any of the arguments of its defenders. Rather feeble methods were pursued, including embargoes on slave-grown sugar [**docs 18, 19**] and campaigns for piece-meal improvements in slave conditions. More effectively, new British acquisitions were made Crown colonies so that planter-control could be avoided.

At the time of the struggle for the Reform Act, a new spirit and new men took control of the movement. A great meeting in May 1830 marked this change. One of the new speakers, advocating immediate abolition, ended: 'The people must emancipate the slaves, for the government never will' (**3**).

As a result, emancipation of the slaves was one of the first reforms tackled by the Whigs after the passage of the 1832 Reform

Act. The middle class, often nonconformist, sector of the electorate saw slavery as both wrong and against their interests. Industrial towns sent members pledged to emancipation. Yorkshire, in particular, with its east coast ports and its woollen industry which did not need plantation colonies either as markets or for raw material, was strongly anti-slavery, and both David Hartley and Wilberforce were members for Hull. The Irish M.P.s, in parliament since the Act of Union and active against the slave trade, were united against this further example of British tyranny. Finally, the West Indian interest, which had been given an unduly powerful political voice by the corruption of the eighteenth-century political system, was especially disliked by the new political groups, which had at the same time been excluded. West Indians had sided with the Tories during the Reform struggle and were ripe for attack.

The Act (3 & 4 Will IV, c 73) 'for the Abolition of Slavery throughout the British Colonies; for promoting the Industry of the Manumitted Slaves; and for compensating the persons hitherto entitled to the Services of Such Slaves' was passed in August 1833, and was to come into effect at the beginning of 1834.

While slavery was technically abolished by this Act, the method of doing so, while ensuring the continuing supply of plantation labour, confused the issue hopelessly, and in the eyes of the freed slaves made the Act a dead letter. Earlier suggested schemes had been even more timid than the final solution, which stated that all slaves over six years old should be 'apprenticed' to their former masters, field slaves to work forty hours a week, and household slaves full time, the former until 1840 and the latter until 1838 (**37, 58**) [**doc. 7**].

As if this was not enough—and it should be remembered that there was no such scheme of semi-slavery introduced in French colonies when their slaves were emancipated in 1848—the principles of the scheme were to be implemented by the local legislatures in each colony, which were of course still completely planter-dominated. Special magistrates, in theory chosen from outside the planter class and to be paid by Great Britain, were given the task of administering the scheme, but these men were badly recruited, underpaid and overworked. Many gave up or, worse, became 'planters' friends' (**37**).

The planters were left with enormous power over their ex-slaves.

The workhouses, which were practically prisons, remained under planter control through the Vestries, and were not placed, as would have been logical, under the Special Magistrates. Any Negro who found himself in a workhouse was liable to flogging every bit as severe as on the plantation under slavery, and might be put to work on a treadmill. At the same time, life for the so-called apprentices was made intolerable by petty restrictions. The slaves were forced to work their forty hours over five or six days, so that they would find it difficult to cultivate their own ground satisfactorily: slaves were paid in kind, and often had trouble selling their goods: supplies of the favoured salt fish were denied the Negroes: manumission was fixed at an impossibly high price. The whole system was so unsatisfactory that it broke down before the date scheduled.

The other feature of the Act is the compensation paid to the owners of slaves. Again it must be noted that French slaveowners were not compensated in 1848. It is surprising that compensation was paid by the British Act since slavery had been abolished explicitly as an evil, and evil presumably should not be compensated. The property defence of slavery can be best appreciated when it is realised that even the reformed parliament was prepared to pay out £20 million to the slaveowners, although the final figure fell somewhat short of this at £18,669,401.

Compensation was calculated on the value of male slaves in each colony, and this varied considerably from colony to colony, from £58 in British Guiana, £56 in Trinidad, £25 in Barbados to £23 in Jamaica. The value of slave children also varied from Trinidad's £22 to Jamaica's £7, while the aged and infirm rated £5 compensation for their owners.

The figures for compensation show the distribution of non-domestic slaves in 1833 (**34**):

Jamaica	254,310 slaves	£5,853,978 compensation
Barbados	66,638 slaves	£1,659,316 compensation
British Guiana	69,579 slaves	£4,068,809 compensation
Trinidad	17,439 slaves	£973,443 compensation
Tobago	9,078 slaves	
Dominica/St Kitts	27,331 slaves	
St Lucia/St Vincent	28,442 slaves	
BRITISH WEST INDIES	512,823 slaves	£15,524,360 compensation

However, it must not be thought that this large total went to either the resident slaveowning planters or even to absentees. The great part of this money was paid to creditor-merchant houses in England, which held enormous mortgages and other debts from planters. Thus the British creditors were able to repatriate quite a reasonable part of their capital from colonies that were approaching more or less complete breakdown, but it was British tax-payers' money that made this possible (**30**).

Emancipation did not produce any immediately disastrous effects, even after the breakdown of the apprentice scheme in 1838 [**doc. 36**]. France, however, did not abolish slavery until 1848 and Spain not finally until the 1880s, so that big slave plantations of Cuba using railways and central factories were established to the great embarrassment of the British colonies, which were able to solve labour problems to some extent by importing coolies from India and the Far East after 1841. The emancipation of the slaves, coupled with the later abandoning of any protective tariffs, left the West Indies defenceless in the struggle for the markets of Britain and Europe.

16 Free Trade

There were two types of duty that affected West Indian sugar producers. The first was the import duty levied on all sugar, and the second was the preferential duty imposed on all sugars other than those from the British West Indies. The latter gave the West Indies a small but valuable advantage over other sugars from within the empire, and an enormous advantage over foreign sugars, which paid a prohibitive 4*d* per lb. above the normal import duties. The British West Indian interest regarded the former duty with dislike, the latter with the strongest approval.

The preferential duty was the key to the survival of the West Indies in the nineteenth century. The twin blows of the abolition of the slave trade and the emancipation of the slaves might have been survived, given reorganisation and an alternative source of labour, but the removal of the preference exposed the British plantations to the immense competition of the huge slave estates of Cuba and Brazil. After the emancipation of the slaves, there was little passion left in the attack on the plantation system, and the free trade movement of mid-century must be seen in purely economic terms of the industrial interests seeking the cheapest raw materials, the widest markets and the cheapest food. Given all these, they hoped to be able to lower prices, increase production and sales, and possibly to lower wages with the cost of living.

Before the American Revolution import duties on sugar had totalled 6·9 shillings per hundredweight. The expenses of the war caused the government to raise the duties to 12·4 shillings by 1782, and at a time when insurance and freight rates were soaring during the war. The duties were raised again in 1792, on the outbreak of the French Revolutionary war, and in 1806 it has been calculated that the duties accounted for 61·7 per cent of the wholesale price of sugar.

The end of the war was the critical time for the sugar colonies. Mauritius, the first serious rival, was now within the empire: foreign sugar would be able to seize the European markets: and the government's decision in 1816 to take off income tax meant that the heavy import duties on commodities, including sugar, would have to continue as a form of indirect taxation. The hard times in the years after the war forced down sugar prices until they were below the combined duties and charges, and the planters began the great sell-out.

Their only hope of survival lay in the preference they received, and this came under serious attack. In the first place, the East Indian interest argued with some force that there was no reason why one part of the empire should have a preference over another, and they were able to utilise the strong feeling against slavery by pointing out that the Indian labour of Mauritius was, at least technically, free. Dr Eric Williams has made great play with this alliance of the 'Saints' and the East India interest (**3**). The combination was a real force, and it is true that Wilberforce considered making Whitmore, the leading East India M.P., his successor as leader of the attack on slavery. In 1825 Mauritius was given equality of duties with the West Indies.

The second attack on the preferences was more all-embracing. This was the Free Trade movement of the early nineteenth century. Adam Smith had stated the case, and as early as 1782 Shelburne was able to say: 'This seems to be the era of protestantism in trade. All Europe appear enlightened, and eager to throw off the vile shackles of oppressive ignorant monopoly' (**6**). In contrast to sugar and corn, cotton, the staple import of the industrial expansion, had never been protected. In 1819 a duty of $\frac{1}{4}d$ per lb was imposed on foreign cotton imports to the disgust of Lancashire, but this could do nothing to boost the tiny share of the cotton imports by then provided by the West Indies.

Huskisson, in his period at the Board of Trade from 1823–8, introduced measures to rationalise the system of duties. It is wrong to call Huskisson an exponent of Free Trade at the expense of Empire, but he succeeded in limiting preferences to the main staple of each area.

In the 1830s the consumption of sugar in England stood at about 20 lb. per capita per annum, and this was the protected market of imperial producers. Foreign workers could buy sugar at $4\frac{1}{2}d$ per lb. compared with the British price of $7\frac{1}{2}d$ per lb., a difference, caused by the preferential duty, which was in effect a large subsidy for the British planters.

In the 1840s the great campaign for a 'free breakfast table' was launched. The Anti-Corn Law League by implication was also anti-sugar preferences. Nevertheless, the rather muted West Indian interest was not finally destroyed until the end of the decade. Who came to their rescue? Surprisingly enough, it was the abolitionists. They realised that if the preference on British sugar was removed, the huge slave plantations of Cuba and Brazil would seize the British market. The planters joined in the decently shocked protests against slavery! From 1844 Peel continued to discriminate against slave-grown sugar to the fury of the industrialists.

But this was only a delay. In Ricardo's words in 1845, 'the ball was rolling, and nothing they could do would suffice to stop it'. In 1846 Lord John Russell gave notice that the Whigs would lower the duties on sugar after the repeal of the Corn Laws. In 1848 the Navigation Laws were swept away. Equalisation of sugar duties was planned for 1851, but a desperate defence was put up by sections of the Tory party under Lord George Bentinck. As a result equalisation was delayed, but there was no stopping it. Disraeli characteristically accepted the inevitable quickly: 'After the immense revolution that has been carried into effect' he said in Parliament in 1853, 'we cannot cling to the rags and tatters of a protective system'. The rags and tatters were duly destroyed in 1854, and it was ironical that this last task should have been carried out by Gladstone, the son of a man who had made his fortune out of his connection with the West Indies.

Imperialism was out of fashion in the mid-nineteenth century, but the reality of a commercial empire was widely supported. The old colonies attracted little sympathy or interest. The Secretary of State for War ran the colonies from 1801–54, and his permanent secretaries for the colonies were the real powers. In this period two men filled this post, James Stephens, an abolitionist, and Herman Merivale, a former Oxford professor of economics (6). Neither of them believed the empire could be maintained by the old devices of protection, but both regarded the empire as a trust which could not be abandoned merely because it had become a liability. This was a modern and responsible view of empire that found few supporters in a country that tended to judge all relationships in terms of the resulting trade. After 1854 the barriers were down. The plantation colonies struggled along using Indian and Chinese labour, but when the great challenge of rival producers came in the 1880s and 1890s they collapsed [**tables 4, 5**].

17 The Empire in Retrospect

In 1750 the plantation empires of the western hemisphere were productive and highly valued in the mother countries. In 1850 their last defences were being destroyed. This book has tried to examine the stages in this transformation, and certain conclusions can be drawn.

The plantation colonies in the Caribbean and on the mainland of North America were regarded primarily as economic assets by the mother countries. This was making an accurate assessment in mid eighteenth century, since these colonies and their attendant trades played a remarkable part in the home economies, as export markets, as producers of needed imports, as employers of shipping, and as generators of a certain amount of capital. They fitted exactly the currently accepted economic thinking, which in fact had developed as a result of the colonies' success.

But the success of these colonies depended on certain pre-conditions: the monopoly of home markets, few rivals, plentiful labour and cheap supplies. These conditions were not to last into the nineteenth century.

As successes the plantations produced sensational profits, and this resulted in intensive monoculture, which was effected by using slave labour from Africa. Slavery made the plantation system possible, but the tensions and the profits combined to create a pattern of absenteeism, particularly in the British Caribbean colonies. In addition, slavery proved a most wasteful labour system, causing a great part of the later debt burden. The concomitant of eighteenth-century slavery was the slave trade, and it was the inhumanity of this aspect that first gave the critics of the system a chance to attack it.

The multiple attacks launched against the plantation empire took some time to be effective, because established ideas always die hard, and at the beginning of the nineteenth century were defended passionately by a threatened and articulate establishment. It is

101

wrong to overestimate the part played by the West India interest in causing this timelag. The interest was noticed and attacked by contemporaries, but its strength lay in the fact that its demands tended to coincide with the Government's thinking about trade, strategy and maritime power and with the ruling classes' belief in the sanctity of property.

The American Revolution and the secession of the American colonies was the blow to the heart of the British plantation empire, since its internal economy was wrecked, and the huge potential of the ex-colonies made it ridiculous to legislate against them for long. The humanitarian, intellectual and artistic activity at the turn of the century militated against the colonies, but the sheer hard facts of economic life were bound to condemn the system of protection, especially when the industrial middle classes found their political voice.

The massive economic and technological changes of the nineteenth century—population growth, industrial expansion, shipping and transport improvements—produced a situation where the remaining plantation colonies were unable to justify a favoured position. They were not big enough, efficient enough or rich enough to warrant attention [**tables 4, 5**]. Little in the nineteenth century operated in favour of the old plantation empire, and the behaviour of West Indians in the preceding generations had forfeited any sympathy that might have been felt for them. The rejection was complete [**doc. 37**].

Part Four

DOCUMENTS

There is no collection of documents covering all aspects of this subject, but relevant material can be found in:

English Historical Documents, vols. IX, X, XI.

E. Donnan, *Documents Illustrative of the Slave Trade*, 4 vols. Washington D.C. 1931.

Basil Davidson, *The African Past*, Longmans, 1964; Penguin African 1966.

George Bennett, ed., *The Concept of Empire*, A. & C. Black, 1953.

Figures given in the tables are abstracted from B. R. Mitchell and P. Deane, *An Abstract of British Historical Statistics*, Cambridge University Press, 1962.

I THE PLANTATIONS

The slave plantation in the Caribbean and the southern colonies of North America was the result of the planters' decision to concentrate on growing cash crops intensively. The more intelligent colonists realised eventually that this may have been a mistake.

document 1
Negro Emancipation No Philanthropy

Instead of becoming, as we might have become, a colony of English, increasing in population, with smaller gains but greater stability, with more of an agricultural and less of a commercial character; we have concentrated a dense population in one spot, and the rest of our estate is waste. The labour of 300 Negroes is brought to bear on a portion of land, which in ordinary cultivation of the richest of European soils would require but ten or twelve efficient labourers. The prospect of high gains from sugar checked the cultivation of minor products.

From a pamphlet, *Negro Emancipation No Philanthropy, a letter to The Duke of Wellington by a Jamaica Landed Proprietor*, London 1830 (**36**).

From an early stage in the plantation period, planters, whether resident or absentee, adopted an extravagant way of life, which quickly saddled them with a burden of debt.

document 2
Tobacco Planters' Extravagance

The tobacco planters live more like country gentlemen or fortune than any other settlers in America; all of them are spread about the country, their labour being mostly by slaves, who are left to overseers; and the masters live in a state of emulation with one another in buildings . . . furniture, wines, dress, diversions etc., and this to a degree, that is rather amazing that they should be able to go on with their plantations at all, than that they should not make additions to them. ... The poverty of the planters here is much talked of, and from thence there has arisen a notion that their husbandry is not profitable: this false idea prevails because of the general luxury and the extravagant way of living that prevails among them ... for men without some rich article of product cannot afford, even with the assistance of credit, to live in such a manner ... that will support such luxury, and pay eight per cent on their debts. What common culture in Europe will do this?

From an anonymous book, *American Husbandry*, 1775.

The combination of a wasteful labour system and an extravagant way of life made the plantations unable to adapt to the loss of slavery and the competition of more efficient producers in the nineteenth century.

document 3

Land, Labour and Profits

The author of this passage was William Sewell, a journalist on the New York Herald Tribune, who had visited the colonies after the emancipation.

Divested of such foreign incumbrances as defects of African character, and other similar stuff and nonsense, it is simply a land question, with which race and colour have nothing whatsoever to do. ... In the West Indies the capitalist refuses to pay high wages; he thinks the control of the labour market is one of his rights. He imagines, upon what ground I cannot comprehend, that farming in these colonies should yield much larger profits than farming anywhere else. He calls it planting, and fancies that there ought to be a wide social distinction between the man who grows cane or cotton and the man who grows potatoes and parsnips. ... The profits of sugar-cultivation, according to the planter's creed, must be large enough to yield the proprietor, though an absentee, a comfortable income, and pay large salaries besides to overseers and attorneys; otherwise estates are abandoned, and the sugar interest is ruined.

From *The Ordeal of Free Labour in the British West Indies* (**34**).

Planters on the French islands, and to some extent in the mainland colonies, tended to be less frequently absentees. They depended entirely on an agent in the mother country to sell their crop and to buy their necessities. This relationship could become very intimate.

A Plantation Order

document 4

I have already by this Conveyance sent to you a Bill of Loading for 6 hogsheads of my Crop of Tobacco and I am now to answer your Letter of the 23rd. of May. I am obliged for your Endeavours to procure me some good red Herrings; but either they do not cure them so well as they did formerly; or, what is more probable, my Taste is altered; so you need not send any more; for I really don't like them; I shall however expect my garden seeds, Cheese, etc. as soon as a new crop comes in with the books I wrote for; and you will be pleased to add the following; viz. Blackstone's Commentary upon the English laws; also one plain hat 6/– 1 laced Ditto and 8 pr of strong Shoes and Pumps for a Boy of eight years old and the same Quantity of Hats and Shoes for two other Boys of 13 and 15 years old.

A Plantation Order from William Nelson, a tobacco planter of Virginia to his English agents, John Norton & Sons, dated 27 August 1768 (**43**).

An inherent problem of the slave plantation was the apparently inevitable wastefulness in the use of labour. Plantations kept Estate Journals to show how the slave labour force was employed from day to day. This is a typical extract from such a journal. 'Drivers' were slaves put in charge of slave gangs. *The First Gang consisted of the strongest men and women: the Second Gang did similar work, but was usually smaller: the Third Gang was for older or sick people: the Fourth Gang was children, employed on collecting food for animals, often known as the 'Hog meat Gang'. The number of watchmen is surprising until one finds that up to 10 per cent of the crop might be lost to pilferers. The large number of children under seven is typical, and it should be noted that the cost of rearing a slave child to the age of fourteen was estimated at £112 in 1831. The 'several brown females' were probably domestics or mistresses of overseers, book-keepers etc. Of 421 slaves listed, 181 are non-workers, about 40 per cent, a figure that tallies with other plantation records.*

document 5

A Planter's Work Force

11 Carpenters	5 Drivers	Also:
7 Coopers	1st Gang – 105	2 Doctors
5 Masons	2nd Gang– 47	1 Doctress
3 Blacksmiths	3rd Gang – 20	2 Midwives
25 Tradesmen	4th Gang – 15	22 Watchmen

Women having 6 children or more exempted from all labour	– 11
Invalids and old people not at work	– 33
Young children under 7 not employed	– 77
Nurses attending on these last two classes	– 18
Several brown females on property exempted from field labour	– 15
Total	– 421

Orange River Estate Journal, 1823: quoted in the *Jamaica Journal* I, No 46.

Where a planter was resident in the 'great house' there would be a domestic staff from 20–40 strong. Document 6 is an example.

Domestic Staff

1 Butler	1 cook	
1 coachman	1 assistant cook	1 waiting-maid
1 postilion	2 footmen or waiting-men	3 house-cleaners
1 helper	1 key or store-keeper	3 washerwomen
		3 seamstresses

In addition, if there were any white children, each child had a nurse and each nurse her assistant boy or girl.

From Long's *History of Jamaica* (**33**).

An argument advanced to justify slavery in the colonies was that there was no other way to keep the labour force working when there was waste land available where they could eke out an alternative living. This belief resulted in the experiment of 'Apprenticeship' after emancipation in 1834. This extract shows this thought process, and suggests an earlier device considered by the government.

Towards Apprenticeship

The great problem to be solved in drawing up any plan for the emancipation of the slaves in our Colonies, is to devise some mode of inducing them when relieved from the fear of the Driver and his whip, to undergo the regular and continuous labour which is indispensable in carrying on the production of Sugar. ... Their (the planters') inability to pay liberal wages seems beyond all question; but even if this were otherwise, the experience of other countries warrants the belief, that while land is so easily obtainable as it is at the moment, even liberal wages would fail to purchase the sort of labour which is required for the cultivation of Sugar ...

I think it would be greatly for the real happiness of the Negroes themselves, if the facility of acquiring land could be so far restrained as to prevent them, on the abolition of slavery, from abandoning their habits of regular industry. Accordingly, it is to the imposition of a considerable tax upon land that I

chiefly look for the means of enabling the planter to continue
his business when emancipation shall have taken place . . .

From an official memorandum by Lord Hawick, Under Secretary
of State for the Colonies, December 1832.

II THE SLAVE TRADE

The price of a slave on the coast of Africa was subject to various factors, such as supply, demand, tribal origin, sex, age and condition of the slave, but it remained fairly constant during the second half of the eighteenth century. The slave was usually paid for in goods, as this extract shows, and thus the trade stimulated industrial production in England.

document 8

Captain Crow's estimate of the price of a slave at Bonny in 1801

> One piece of Chintz, eighteen yards long;
> One piece of Baft, eighteen yards long;
> One piece of Chelloe, eighteen yards long;
> One piece of Bandanoe, seven handkerchiefs;
> One piece of Niccannee, fourteen yards long;
> One piece of Cushtae, fourteen yards long;
> One piece of Photae, fourteen yards long;
> Three pieces of Romalls, forty-five handkerchiefs;
> One large brass pan, two muskets;
> Twenty-five kegs of powder, one hundred flints;
> Two bags of shots, Twenty knives;
> Four iron pots, four hats, four caps;
> Four cutlasses, six hundred bunches of beads,
>   fourteen gallons of brandy.

These articles cost about £25, so that the reader will see we did not procure negroes (as many have supposed) for nothing.

From *Trade Winds* (**18**).

The slave trade was in theory very profitable, but the traders also ran many risks, including mutiny by the slaves. For this reason the slavers carried large crews. This extract describes such an event:

Revolt at Sea

By a Vessel lately arrived here from the West-Indies, we have
Advice, that a Ship belonging to Liverpool coming from the
Coast of Africa, with about 350 Slaves on board, and when in
Sight of the Island Guardaloupe, the Slaves, as 'tis supposed,
being admitted to come upon Deck to air themselves, took an
Opportunity on the 28th of May ... and kill'd the Master
and Mate of the Ship, and threw fifteen of the Men overboard,
after which they sent the Boat with two white Lads and three
or four others to discover what Land it was, meanwhile the
Ship drove to the Leeward, which gave the Lads an Opportunity
to discover the Affair to the Commandant of that Quarter of
the Island, who immediately raised about 100 Men, and put
them on board a Sloop, who went in Pursuit of the Ship, and
in a few Hours took her and carried her into Port Louis.

From *The Boston Post Boy*, 25 June 1750 quoted (**26**).

*An argument frequently used by abolitionists in the debates on the slave
trade was that the trade demoralised Africans on the coast and deep into
the continent, and that the frequent wars were the result of the European
demand for slaves and their readiness to supply dependent kingdoms
with firearms. This extract shows the truth of their contention. Wadström
was a Swedish scientist who visited Africa in 1787-8.*

Effects of Slaving in Africa

The Wars which the inhabitants of the interior parts of the
country, beyond Senegal, Gambia, and Sierra Leona (sic),
carry on with each other, are chiefly of a predatory nature, and
owe their origin to the yearly number of slaves, which the
Mandingoes, or the inland traders suppose will be wanted by
the vessels that will arrive on the coast. Indeed these predatory
incursions depend so much on the demand for slaves, that if in
any one year there be a greater concourse of European ships

than usual, it is observed that a much greater number of captives from the interior is brought to market the next

The Moors, who inhabit the countries on the north of the River Senegal, are particularly infamous for their predatory Wars . . . The French, to encourage them in it, make annual presents to the Moorish kings. These are given them under certain conditions, first, that their subjects shall not carry any of their gum to the English at Portendic; and, secondly, that they shall be ready on all occasions, to furnish slaves. To enable them to fulfil this last article, they never fail to supply them with ammunition, guns, and other instruments of War.

From C. B. Wadström, *Observations on the Slave Trade*, London, 1789 (**26**).

From an early date there were criticisms of the trade as cruel, but before the wave of humanitarianism at the end of the eighteenth century these attacks were waved to one side on empirical grounds. These two extracts are typical:

document 11

Justifications of the Slave Trade
The Traders' Plea

Tho' to traffic in human creatures, may at first seem barbarous, inhuman, and unnatural; yet the traders herein have as much to plead in their own excuse, as can be said for some other branches of trade, namely, the *advantage* of it. In a word, from this trade proceed benefits, far outweighing all, either real or pretended mischiefs and inconveniencies.

From W. Snelgrave, *A New Account of Guinea and the Slave Trade* (**3**).

A Speech in Parliament by Temple Luttrell, May 1777 (extract)

Some gentlemen may, indeed, object to the slave trade as inhuman and impious; let us consider that if our colonies are to be maintained and cultivated, which can only be done by African negroes, it is surely better to supply ourselves with those labourers in British bottoms, than purchase them through the medium of French, Dutch, or Danish factors.

From *Parliamentary History* xix, 305, 23 May 1777 (**3**).

III SLAVERY

The debate on slavery is marked by its ingenuity and passion on both sides. Personal interest and prejudice frequently clouded the issue, but certain writers in England saw that the institution was an evil from an early date. This is one such clear statement.

Horace Walpole to Sir Horace Mann
document 13

I am a bad Englishman, because I think the advantages of commerce are dearly bought for some by the lives of many more . . . But every age has some ostentatious system to excuse the havoc it commits. Conquest, honour, chivalry, religion, balance of power, commerce, no matter what, mankind must bleed, and take a term for a reason.

From a letter, dated 26 May 1762 (**51**).

The debate in miniature can be savoured in this extract from Boswell's Life of Johnson, *since the two men found themselves strongly opposed.*

Dr Johnson's Views
document 14

The passage is dated 1777, Johnson being 68.

He had always been very zealous against slavery in every form, in which I with all deference thought that he discovered a zeal without knowledge. Upon one occasion, when in company with some very grave men at Oxford, his toast was: 'Here's to the next insurrection of the negroes in the West Indies.' His violent prejudice against our West Indian and American settlers appeared whenever there was an opportunity. Towards the conclusion of his 'Taxation no Tyranny', he says, 'How is it that we hear the loudest *yelps* for liberty among the drivers of negroes?'

The Argument dictated by Dr Johnson was as follows:
'It must be agreed that in most ages many countries have had part of their inhabitants in a state of slavery; yet it may be doubted whether slavery can ever be supposed the natural condition of man. It is impossible not to conceive that men in their original state were equal; and very difficult to imagine how one would be subjected to another but by violent compulsion. An individual may, indeed, forfeit his liberty by a crime; but he cannot by that crime forfeit the liberty of his children. What is true of a criminal seems true likewise of a captive. . . .
'The laws of Jamaica afford a negro no redress. His colour is considered as a sufficient testimony against him. It is to be lamented that moral right should ever give way to political convenience. But if temptations of interest are sometimes too strong for human virtue, let us at least retain a virtue where there is no temptation to quit it.'
I record Dr Johnson's argument fairly upon this particular case; where, perhaps, he was in the right. *But I beg leave to enter my most solemn protest against his general doctrine with respect to the slave trade.* For I will resolutely say, that his unfavourable notion of it was owing to prejudice, and imperfect or false information. The wild and dangerous attempt which has for some time been persisted in to obtain an act of our legislature, to abolish so very important and necessary a branch of commercial interest, must have been crushed at once, had not the insignificance of the zealots who vainly took the lead in it made the vast body of planters, merchants, and others, whose immense properties are involved in that trade, reasonably enough suppose that there could be no danger. The encouragement which the attempt has received excites my wonder and indignation; and though some men of superior abilities have supported it, whether from a love of temporary popularity when prosperous, or a love of general mischief when desperate, my opinion is unshaken. To abolish a *status*, which in all ages God has sanctioned, and man has continued, would not only be *robbery* to an innumerable class of our fellow-subjects, but it would be extreme cruelty to the African savages, a portion of whom it saves from massacre, or intolerable bondage in their own country, and introduces into a much happier state of life; especially now when their

116

passage to the West Indies and their treatment there is humanely regulated. To abolish that trade would be to—shut the gates of mercy on mankind.

Whatever may have passed elsewhere concerning it, the House of Lords is wise and independent. . . .

From James Boswell's *The Life of Samuel Johnson*, John Murray, 1839, vol. 7.

The planters and their allies fell back on other arguments. One was that the slaves were not unhappy, and that their conditions compared favourably with those of English workers. Some writers could become poetic on this theme.

document 15

'The Happy Negro'

And now the happy negro homeward goes,
Contented as the honey-laden bee,
Because his heart no earthly sorrow knows.
Deluded sons of Britain! Would that ye,
The proud, the brave, the omnipotent, the free,
Beheld him seated at his ample meal,
With all his children smiling at his knee!
Then would ye know the nature of his weal,
And honestly confirm, the truth of this appeal.

William Hosack in *The Jamaica Monthly Magazine*, xi, October 1833 (**36**).

A popular argument to defend the institution was that the Negro was an inferior being, unfitted for freedom. Eminent support for this view was not difficult to find.

document 16

From David Hume, 'Of National Characters', 1753

I am apt to suspect the Negroes to be naturally inferior to the Whites. There scarcely ever was a civilised nation of that complexion, nor ever any individual, eminent either in action or speculation. No ingenious manufactures among them, no arts, no sciences. On the other hand, the most rude and barbarous of all the Whites, such as the ancient Germans, the present Tartars, have still something eminent about them in their valour, form of government, or some other particular. Such a uniform and constant difference could not happen, in so many countries and ages, if nature had not made an original distribution between these breeds of men. ... In Jamaica, indeed, they talk of one Negro (Francis Williams) as a man of parts and learning; but it is likely he is admired for slender accomplishments, like a parrot who speaks a few words plainly.

Quoted (34).

Some planters were able to argue, with justification, that a slave was well cared for, since anything else would be economically stupid. This extract is from a planter who had been shrewd and successful, but who had retired to England, and wrote regularly to his manager.

document 17

A Planter's Care

It is unnecessary, I flatter myself, to say a word respecting the care of my slaves and stock—your own good sense must tell you they are the sinews of a plantation and must claim your particular care and attention. Humanity tempered with justice towards the former must ever be exercised, and when sick I am satisfied they will experience every kindness from you, they surely deserve it, being the very means of our support. The latter must be kept clean from ticks.

From a letter from John Pinney to his manager in Nevis.

As the debates on the slaves reached a pitch in England planters had good reason for appearing to treat slaves well. The same planter wrote later to his manager about the visit to his estate of a certain Mr Wedgwood, a friend of Wilberforce.

Do not suffer a negro to be corrected in his presence, or so near for him to hear the whip . . . point out the comforts the negroes enjoy beyond the poor in this country, drawing a comparison between the climates—show him the property they possess in goats, hogs, and poultry, and their negro-ground. By this means he will leave the island possessed with favourable sentiments.

Quoted (30).

In the campaign against slavery the emancipationists tried to introduce an embargo on slave-grown sugar by encouraging consumers in England to use sugar grown in the East by free labour. Document 18 shows one way the appeal was launched, and Document 19 suggests that the campaign had some effect.

The Negro Slave's Complaint

document 18

And now, massa, you be de *friend of freedom*, good man, pity poor Negro, me beg buy the East Sugar, no slave sugar, de free, and den my massa vill tink and say, ve no much sell de slave sugar, slaves must be no slaves, must be free, and ve pay de vages, and den vill vork villing and do more work, and ve den sell more *sugar*, and get more of de money.—De men at de East be vise men, and de vise men at de East no slave—make sugar free, free, free.

From *The Negro Slave's Complaint to Humanity*, an undated pamphlet in the Wilberforce Museum, Hull (3).

Against the Embargo on Sugar

document 19

The combination entered into by a set of enthusiasts in this country to leave off the use of sugar, in order, as they say, to destroy the slave trade, by slow but certain means, have had, united with the high price of the article, a great effect on the consumption. Some will leave it off under the idea they are benefiting a large body of fellow creatures, and thousands will make use of a like plea to cover a parsimonious disposition, so in both cases the poor planter will be the sufferer.

From a letter by John Pinney, on the embargo on Slave Sugar, dated 1792 (**30**).

IV WAR AIMS IN THE CARIBBEAN

War in the Caribbean was made more difficult by the selfish attitude of the colonists who were concerned only with their own interests and security. Their cause was supported in England by opponents of a 'continental' war, which they argued was fought purely in the Hanoverian interest.

document 20

Suggested Strategy

By a well-managed descent upon their sugar-islands, of which they are as tender as the apple of their eye, we should at once ruin them, and promote the welfare of our own for many years. This might be done by only destroying their ingenios or sugar-works, and carrying off their slaves.

From a pamphlet, *The Present Ruinous Land-War proved to be a Hanoverian War*, London 1745.

The government appears to have been well aware of the interests behind this line of argument, as this extract from correspondence between Newcastle and Hardwicke shows. The letters are discussing Martinique, and were written in 1762.

document 21

Conflicting Interests

Newcastle to Hardwicke

They (the planters) wished to have had it destroyed, their negroes taken, and the whole demolished. But it is always a good thing to have in hand.

Hardwicke's reply

They have but one point in view, which is how it may affect their particular interest; and they wish all colonies destroyed but that wherein they are particularly interested, in order to raise the market for their own commodities.

Extracts from correspondence between Newcastle and Hardwicke, 1762.

The West India policy of damaging raids of course worked both ways, and planters on the smaller islands were terrified of French attacks. These extracts from John Pinney's letters home from Nevis show why.

document 22

Local Defences

It was with concern I observed the countenances and actions of some men, who seemed pleased at the approaching period (of French invasion); I believe they flattered themselves it would be a short way of extinguishing the claims of those troublesome fellows, Creditors. . . .

Our whole force consisted in less than 300 militia, indifferently armed and trained, that we had no post of any strength to retire to and that if we had time to throw up a redoubt, it must be defended by the planters and inhabitants, who would of course be thereby obliged to abandon their lives, families and estates to the mercy of a soldiery irritated by an ill-judged resistance. . . . It was therefore thought that any opposition would be little better than madness.

Extracts from letters of John Pinney, dated 1778 (**30**).

The climax of the clash between West Indian interests and wider concerns came over the famous Canada versus Guadeloupe controversy at the end of the Seven Years War. There was an enormous pamphlet dialogue (some of which can be found in E.H.D. vol X), but these extracts show the government itself was in little doubt, and that the West Indian interest was not important in deciding the issue.

Canada or Guadaloupe?

1. NEWCASTLE'S 'MEMORANDUMS FOR THE KING': 14 OCTOBER 1760

Alderman Baker's reasoning:	About keeping Canada or the Newfoundland fishery; and Cape Breton or Guadeloupe. Senegal etc.

The keeping of Canada the most necessary for preserving the peace; which cannot be done whilst Canada and those parts are divided between two rival Powers, England and France, as the Indians will always be stirr'd up one against the other.

The keeping of the others might be more beneficial in point of trade; but the others for the preservation of the peace.

2. BAKER TO NEWCASTLE: 13 APRIL 1761

Guadeloupe is well worthy to be retained if possible, but not in an equal degree with North America, and if somewhat must be given up this island seems the fittest.

The Neutrall Islands are very differently circumstanced, they are of right belonging to Great Britain, and ought to be ceded as such, and be immediately possest and planted by the English ... The English want more sugar land to plant not only to supply foreign markets, but also to encrease the quantity for home consumption, and thereby reduce the price of a commodity now become of general and necessary use ...

3. CHESTERFIELD TO NEWCASTLE: 30 NOVEMBER 1760

I think we should keep Quebec and Canada as preventives of future war, and for the rest scramble and negotiate as well as we can. The French I am persuaded would more willingly give up Canada than Guadeloupe, as they have no great notion of that furr trade and indeed never received any great returns from it; but Guadeloupe is a much more lucrative possession.

4. HARDWICKE TO NEWCASTLE: 2 APRIL 1762

As to the retention of conquests, Mr. Pitt made North-America entirely his object. Some of his enemies objected to him that he did this out of partiality to his friend, Beckford, and out of condescension to the particular interests of our Sugar Colonies; but in that I suppose they do him wrong . . .

It will be said that none of these objections (produce, population, expense) occur against the French Sugar Colonies. They are fertile countries; may be easily peopled, and, being islands, be easily defended, particularly by your squadrons now in use to be sent annually. They must take all the necessaries of life from the Mother Country, as your own islands now do. The sugar trade is a most profitable one, and you may engross almost the whole of it, and serve all the European markets. To defend them you will not want troops, or, at the most, a very few.

A great deal of this reasoning has already been retail'd in the pamphlets; but when it was confin'd to Guadeloupe only, it did not carry so great weight, for France still remain'd in possession of the greater part. But it will come with redoubled force, now you have acquired the possession of *all* the Caribbee Islands, especially if what is said be true *that they are the key of the whole West-Indies*. I am very glad that Rodney did not put this into his public letter.

Quoted (51).

V THE WEST INDIAN INTERESTS

The plantation colonies were highly prized, almost as a point of dogma, by both France and England in the mid-eighteenth century. These two extracts, almost exactly contemporary, the first English, the second French, speak the same language. It should be mentioned here that Abbé Raynal, the author of Document 25, was a pioneer of the French movement against slavery, his book being translated into English in 1777.

The Colonial Empire as a Source of Wealth
document 24

The most approved Judges of the Commercial Interests of these Kingdoms have been of the opinion that our West-India and African Trades are the most nationally beneficial of any we carry on. It is also allowed on all Hands that the Trade to Africa is the Branch which renders our American Colonies and Plantations so advantageous to Great Britain: that Traffic only affording our Planters a constant supply of Negro Servants for the Culture of their Lands in the Produce of Sugars, Tobacco, Rice, Rum, Cotton, Fustick, Pimento and all our other Plantation Produce: so that the extensive Employment of our Shipping in, to, and from America, the great Brood of Seamen consequent thereupon, and the daily Bread of the most considerable of our British Manufactures, are owing primarily to the Labour of Negroes; who, as they were the first happy instruments of raising our Plantations, so their Labour only can support and preserve them, and render them still more and more profitable to their Mother-Kingdom. The Negroe-Trade therefore, and the natural consequences resulting from it, may be justly esteemed an inexhaustible Fund of Wealth and Naval Power to this Nation.

From a pamphlet published in London in 1749 (3).

Abbé Raynal on the French West Indies, 1750

The labours of the people settled in these islands are the sole bases of the African trade; they extend the fisheries and culture of North America, afford a good market for the manufactures of Asia, and double, perhaps treble, the activity of all Europe. They may now be considered the principal cause of the rapid motion which now agitates the universe. This ferment must increase, in proportion as cultures, that are so capable of being extended, shall approach nearer to their higher degree of perfection.

Quoted (1).

The famous French Encyclopédie *stated the protectionist view that this wealth should be regulated for the benefit of the mother country.*

A French View of Empire

Les colonies n'étant établies que pour l'utilité de la metropole, il s'ensuit:

1. Qu'elles doivent être sous sa dépendance immédiate et par conséquent sous sa protection;

2. Que le commerce doit en être exclusif aux fondateurs.

From *L'Encyclopédie,* 1751–68 (4).

In England, and to a lesser degree in France, the planters organised themselves to exert pressure on their governments to protect a system that gave them a monopoly of the home market. These two extracts show their aims and methods.

The Planters' Club

The sugar planters that Reside in England being desirous to promote the Interest of the Sugar Colonys in every Branch of it, as far as Lay in their Power; and to put a stop to many abuses that had crept into the Sugar Trade, thought that the first step to be taken for promoting these ends, would be for the Gentlemen belonging to the several Islands, to Unite into one Body; and Accordingly they did some Years ago, form themselves into a Society in London, which takes the name of the Planters' Club.

From a letter to the Council of Montserrat, dated 16 October 1745, signed by 28 names, including William Beckford. Colonial Office Papers 177 (**67**).

Merchants' Pressure on M.P.s

The printed case has been sent to the respective house of every Member of Parliament in Town. The Agents, Planters and Merchants, have also agreed and divided themselves into several small parties to attend upon the several Members, and many of them have already been addressed upon the Subject and every one of them will be solicited personally, before the Bill comes into the House. All people that have any Interest with such as have Influence with Members are also Courted, and People in general seem to think as we do, in opposition to the Bill. Copies of the case have also been dispersed to the several sea-ports of the Kingdom, besides publishing it in the Evening Post, and nothing shall be wanted to make the clamour popular, and if possible to get this d—d Bill as much abhorred as the Excise Scheme.

From a letter from the firm of Lascelles and Maxwell to Barbados concerning the 1743 proposal to levy a duty of 2s 6d per cwt on imported sugar (**67**).

F

Attacks on the institution of slavery came from many quarters at the end of the eighteenth century. The system of colonial protection, in which slavery played so integral a part, was attacked by economists, notably Dean Tucker and Adam Smith.

document 29

Adam Smith on the Economic Aspect

The maintenance of this monopoly has hitherto been the principal, or more properly the sole end and purpose of the dominion which Great Britain assumes over her colonies. ... The expence of the ordinary peace establishment of the colonies amounted, before the commencement of the present disturbances, to the pay of twenty regiments of foot; ... to the expence of a very considerable naval force which was constantly kept up, in order to guard, from the smuggling vessels of other nations, the immense coast of North America, and that of our West Indian islands. The whole expence of this peace establishment was a charge upon the revenue of Great Britain, and was, at the same time, the smallest part of what the dominion of the colonies has cost the mother country. ... We must add to it, in particular, the whole expence of the late war, and a great part of the war which preceded it. The late war was altogether a colony quarrel, and the whole expence of it, in whatever part of the world it had been laid out, whether in Germany or the East Indies, ought justly to be stated to the account of the colonies. It amounted to more than ninety million pounds sterling. ... The Spanish war which began in 1739, was principally a colony quarrel. ... The whole expence is, in reality, a bounty which has been given in order to support a monopoly. The pretended purpose of it was to encourage the manufactures, and to increase the commerce of Great Britain. But its real effect had been to raise the rate of mercantile profit, and to enable our merchants to turn into a branch of trade, of which the returns are more slow and distant than those of the greater part of other trades, a greater proportion of their capital than they would otherwise have done; two events which if a bounty could have prevented, it might perhaps have been very worth while to give such a bounty.

Under the present system of management, therefore, Great Britain derives nothing but loss from the dominion which she assumes over her colonies.

From Adam Smith, *An Inquiry into the Nature and Causes of the Wealth of Nations*, book IV, chap. 7: iii.

The stated principles of the French Revolution were completely opposed to slavery. This was put vividly by Robespierre in this extract.

document 30

Robespierre on Political Morality

What is our aim? The quiet enjoyment of liberty and equality; the reign of that eternal justice whose laws are written, not on marble or stone, but in the heart of every man, even in that of the slave who forgets and the tyrant who denies them. We desire an order of things ... in which there are no distinctions but such as arise on a basis of equality; ... in which the country guarantees the well-being of every individual ... and commerce is the source of public wealth, not merely the monstrous growth of a few private fortunes. ... For the pettiness of the so-called great we would substitute the grandeur of humanity ... In a word, we wish to fulfil the vows of nature, to accomplish the destinies of humanity ... May France, once notorious for its slavery, now eclipse the glory of all the free peoples of history, and become the model of the nations, the terror of the oppressors, the consolation of the oppressed, the ornament of the universe; and may we, whilst we seal our work with our blood, see at least the first rays of the dawn of universal felicity. That is our ambition: that is our aim.

From Robespierre's Report of 5 February 1794, 'On the principles of political morality that ought to guide the Convention' (quoted by J. M. Thompson: *Leaders of the French Revolution*, Blackwell, 1948).

It is sad to follow the practical application of these ideas. The French planters seemed to have over-estimated their security, as this extract shows.

The Dangers of Liberty

Even at table, surrounded by mulattoes and negroes, they indulge themselves in the most imprudent discussions on liberty etc. To discuss 'The Rights of Man' before such people —what is it but to teach them that power dwells with strength, and strength with numbers?

An extract from a letter of Baron de Wimpffen, 1790 (**1**).

After the disasters in Saint Domingue and the establishment of the more practical and reactionary government of Napoleon in France, a different tone appears in French governmental thinking about slavery.

Leclerc's Secret Orders

As regards the return of the blacks to the old regime, the bloody struggle out of which you have just come victorious with glory commands us to use the utmost caution. . . . For some time yet vigilance, order, a discipline at once rural and military, must take the place of the positive and pronounced slavery of the coloured people of your colony. Especially the master's good usage must attach them to his rule . . . then the moment will have arrived for making them return to their original condition, from which it was disastrous to draw them.

From instructions sent by Decrès, Minister of Marine and in charge of French colonies, to General Leclerc, dated 14 June 1802 (**41**).

*Writers and artists added their weight to the growing feelings against
the system of slavery, to some extent with the greatest effect since their
impact was pure and emotional.*

The Little Black Boy

My mother bore me in the southern wild,
And I am black, but O my soul is white;
White as an angel is the English child,
But I am black, as if bereav'd of light.

My mother taught me underneath a tree,
And, sitting down before the heat of day,
She took me on her lap and kissèd me,
And, pointing to the east, began to say:

Look on the rising sun, there God does live,
And gives His light, and gives His heat away;
And flowers and trees and beasts and men receive
Comfort in morning, joy in the noonday.

And we are put on earth a little space,
That we may learn to bear the beams of love;
And these black bodies and this sunburnt face
Is but a cloud, and like a shady grove.

For when our souls have learn'd the heat to bear,
The cloud will vanish, we shall hear His voice,
Saying: 'Come out from the grove, My love and care,
And round My golden tent like lambs rejoice.'

Thus did my mother say, and kissèd me;
And thus I say to little English boy,
When I from black, and he from white cloud free,
And round the tent of God like lambs we joy,

I'll shade him from the heat, till he can bear
To lean in joy upon His Father's knee;
And then I'll stand and stroke his silver hair,
And be like him, and he will then love me.

William Blake, in *Songs of Innocence*, 1789.

By the nineteenth century the colonies were being regarded in the same light as the unreformed parliament and the Corn Laws, as rackets run for the benefit of the rich. This extract illustrates this attitude.

document 34

James Mill on Exploitation

It never ought to be forgotten, that, in every country, there is 'a Few', and there is 'a Many'; that in all countries in which the government is not very good, the interest of 'the Few' prevails over the interest of 'the Many,' and is promoted at their expence. 'The Few' is the part that governs; 'the Many' the part that is governed. It is according to the interest of 'the Few' that colonies should be cultivated. This, if it is true, accounts for the attachment which most of the countries, that is, of the governments of modern Europe, have displayed to colonies.

... There is not one of the colonies but what augments the number of places. There are governorships and judgeships, and a long train of *et ceteras*; and above all, there is not one of them but what requires an additional number of troops, and an additional portion of navy,—that is of great importance. In every additional portion of the army and navy, beside the glory of the thing, there are generalships, and colonelships, and captainships, and lieutenantships, and in the equipping and supplying of additional portions of army and navy, there are always gains, which may be thrown in the way of a friend. All this is enough to account for a very considerable quantity of affection maintained towards colonies. ...

Of the proposition, that colonies are a grand source of wars, and of additional expence in wars ... it is not probable that much proof will be required. ...

An extract of the entry 'Colony' by James Mill in the 1824 edition of the *Encyclopaedia Brittanica*.

In addition there was the vein of humanitarian thinking implied in the Evangelical and Non-conformist Christian missions that became a feature of the West Indies about the turn of the century. Christianity and slavery were clearly incompatible, and the planters' suspicions of the preachers were intensified by the involvement of missionaries in some slave troubles. This extract shows how strong West Indian feeling was against the Methodists.

The Methodists

document 35

Shooting is . . . too honourable a death for men whose conduct has occasioned so much bloodshed, and the loss of so much property. There are fine hanging woods in St James and Trelawnay, and we do sincerely hope, that the bodies of all the Methodist preachers who may be convicted of sedition, may diversify the scene.

From the Jamaican newspaper *The Courant*, 6 January 1832 (**36**).

From the turn of the century landowners in the Caribbean began to sell out. This became more difficult, as offers near the estimated values of the estates could not be found. Each blow at the plantation system added to the gloom of the planters: abolition of the slave trade, emancipation of the slaves, and finally the removal of all preferences for West Indian or imperial sugar. These extracts of letters from a diligent planter on Nevis to his creditors, the Pinneys of Bristol, show the despondency.

document 36

Depression Sets In

I wish I had the money in America or I could dispose of them (his estates) at a loss. I should be happy, for what is to become of my large family God knows, and the moment emancipation takes place there will be an end to these colonies, you need not send another ship for sugars.

An extract from a letter from Peter Huggins to the firm of Pinney, dated 1831 (**30**).

document 37

Heading for Ruin

I am sorry to say that our crop will not bear the expense of labour and contingent expenses. If the Government of Her Majesty do not take our deplorable condition into consideration I see nothing but ruin. . . . Every day I see things getting worse and worse. The negroes won't work, they want high wages, do as little work as they can, knock off at three o'clock and call it a day's work. I assure you I am quite a slave and the man that is not must be ruined.

Peter Huggins to the firm of Pinney, dated 12 July 1852 (**30**).

The wheel had turned with a vengeance. The planter was a slave.

Table 1: Notes

Table 1 compares the value of sugar and cotton imports between 1750 and 1850. The figures are in £1,000s—thus sugar imports in 1750 were valued at £1,270,000.

The *value* of sugar imports increased from 1763, reaching a temporary peak just before the American Revolution in 1776. The war caused a fall in imports since Great Britain lost control of the sea, but the value of imports picked up strongly until the outbreak of the French Revolutionary wars from 1792. During these wars the value of sugar imports soared, giving the plantation colonies a last lease of life. From 1815 the sugar imported to Great Britain came increasingly from areas other than the British West Indies, especially after the Free Trade legislation of 1846–54.

Mitchell and Deane's figures for cotton imports begin from 1772, and it should be remembered that the B.W.I. colonies produced the greater part of the imports until the 1790's, but it is only after this date that cotton imports become really significant. Sugar continues to compare with cotton until about 1825.

It is interesting to compare the rate of growth in the value of these imports in this period. Sugar doubles between 1750 and 1770, and again by the turn of the century, and once again with the 'freeing' of sugar at the end of the period—three times in the period under review. Cotton, beginning at a very low figure, doubles between 1772 and 1782, and redoubles in 1787, 1799, by about 1808, 1824, 1834 and 1844—seven times in the period.

Table 1 Imports of Cotton and Sugar, in £1,000s

	SUGAR	COTTON
1750	1,270	
1751	1,147	
1752	1,161	
1753	1,551	
1754	1,178	
1755	1,636	
1756	1,513	
1757	755	

	SUGAR	COTTON
1758	1,661	
1759	1,814	
1760	1,799	
1761	2,126	
1762	1,996	
1763	2,422	
1764	1,978	
1765	1,652	
1766	2,052	
1767	2,103	
1768	2,203	
1769	2,205	
1770	2,436	
1771	1,977	
1772	2,429	160
773	1,963	93
1774	2,704	178
1775	2,664	204
1776	2,298	194
1777	1,837	218
1778	1,933	187
1779	1,983	138
1780	1,813	211
1781	1,411	159
1782	1,799	357
1783	2,061	300
1784	2,451	349
1785	2,855	543
1786	2,072	568
1787	2,474	665
1788	2,620	589
1789	2,488	917
1790	2,402	875
1791	2,304	783
1792	2,721	1,129
1793	2,955	632
1794	3,348	780
1795	2,901	859

	SUGAR	COTTON
1796	3,057	1,027
1797	2,885	1,049
1798	3,663	1,049
1799	4,637	1,430
1800	4,301	1,848
1801	5,436	1,629
1802	5,878	2,088
1803	4,356	1,871
1804	4,440	2,156
1805	4,337	2,081
1806	5,205	2,034
1807	4,972	2,610
1808	5,128	1,471
1809	5,451	3,117
1810	6,558	4,555
1811	5,346	3,148
1812	5,033	2,131
1813	—	—
1814	5,493	2,031
1815	5,440	3,336
1816	5,141	3,152
1817	5,189	4,158
1818	5,418	5,764
1819	5,568	4,869
1820	5,553	4,934
1821	5,739	4,347
1822	4,977	4,735
1823	5,477	6,242
1824	5,733	4,865
1825	5,056	7,406
1826	5,603	5,727
1827	5,328	8,964
1828	6,312	7,483
1829	6,280	7,289
1830	6,857	8,786
1831	7,534	9,612
1832	6,784	9,483
1833	6,627	10,019

	SUGAR	COTTON
1834	6,650	10,897
1835	6,214	12,071
1836	6,519	13,352
1837	6,286	13,483
1838	7,040	16,656
1839	6,618	12,705
1840	5,698	19,500
1841	6,845	15,948
1842	6,738	17,244
1843	7,139	22,279
1844	6,929	21,239
1845	8,762	23,950
1846	8,150	15,376
1847	11,742	15,377
1848	10,185	23,405
1849	10,521	24,901
1850	9,787	21,532
1851	12,276	24,582
1852	10,448	30,326
1853	11,043	28,883
1854	13,764	28,657

Table 2 Cotton Exports: 1750–1829

Table 2 shows the value of exported cotton textiles, which are contrasted with the value of exported woollen textiles. The latter are indicated by showing the ten year average figure. While woollen textile exports remain fairly steady throughout the period, cotton makes the most sensational advance. This development in itself explains the change in attitude towards the plantation colonies, which increasingly fail to be significant as producers of raw material or as markets.

It will be noted that the rapid development of the cotton exports occurs from the 1790s, resulting in part from the invention of the saw gin by Eli Whitney and the opening up of the cotton lands of the southern United States by slave plantations. Clearly developments in trans-Atlantic shipping, machinery, growth of population in England, and domestic transport all played their part.

Table 2 Cotton Exports in £1,000s

	COTTON	WOOL (10 YEAR AVERAGE)
1750	73	
	115	
	85	
	65	
	101	
	124	
	116	
	113	
	167	
	151	
1760	183	4,300
	399	
	200	
	249	
	224	
	273	
	213	
	212	

	COTTON	WOOL (10 YEAR AVERAGE)
1770	199	4,450
	311	
	245	
	181	
	258	
	252	
	289	
	246	
	191	
1780	303	4,000
	306	
	296	
	405	
	746	
	848	
	826	
	872	
	1,025	
	1,150	
	1,089	
1790	1,456	3,500
	1,637	
	1,922	
	1,653	
	2,280	
	2,309	
	3,061	
	2,464	
	3,622	
1800	3,859	5,150
	6,941	
	7,667	
	7,143	
	8,792	
	9,653	
	0,482	
	0,287	

	COTTON	WOOL (10 YEAR AVERAGE)
	13,411	
	19,732	
1810	19,109	6,000
	19,109	
	12,261	
	16,939	
	—	
	17,869	
	22,555	
	17,564	
	21,259	
	22,589	
	18,282	
1820	22,532	5,600
	23,542	
	26,911	
	26,545	
	30,156	
	29,495	
	25,194	
	33,183	
	33,476	
1829	37,269	5,450

Table 3 Notes

With the dramatic expansion of British industry in the closing decades of the eighteenth century, the search for markets became of the greatest importance. Table 3 shows the value of British exports to various key regions during the period that Protection was coming under scrutiny.

Points to note:

(*a*) The importance of Europe as a market, especially immediately after 1815 with the return of peace. In 1822 the two European markets absorbed nearly 60 per cent of the exports. This market had grown by 400 per cent in these forty years.

(*b*) The Asian market was buoyant, but it had not grown significantly between 1790 and 1820, although the last two years on this table indicate a new 'take-off.'

(*c*) The African market contracted sharply after the abolition of the slave trade in 1807, and an alternative market on that continent had not yet been developed.

(*d*) The United States had proved itself to be an important market, recovering quickly from the country's departure from the imperial trade system. The market was somewhat static from 1800 to 1822. The War of 1812 should be noticed accounting for the virtual stopping of trade in 1814. This interruption was brief, and 1815's figures made up for the loss, although it seems that Canada may have made a permanent advance as a result of the war.

(*e*) South America developed very rapidly as a market after the independence of the republics in the first decades of the century, and outstripping the West Indies by the end of this period.

(*f*) The British West Indies were still a sound market, the value of exports to them in this period more than trebling. But relatively they were less important as the United States, South America and Asia all equalled them, and hinted at a greater potential by 1822.

Table 3 Great Britain Exports (including Re-exports) in £1,000s (°10 year averages in £ million)

	N.EUROPE	S.EUROPE	ASIA	AFRICA	U.S.A.	B.W.I.	For w.i./s.am.
1780	4,270	922	1,116	196	829	1,752	127
	3,870	840	595	313	855	1,024	31
	4,400	1,262	1,468	352	267	1,272	229
	3,665	2,050	701	788	1,003	1,797	61
	3,826	2,433	731	524	3,679	1,370	31

	N.EUROPE	S.EUROPE	ASIA	AFRICA	U.S.A.	B.W.I.	For W.I./S.AM.
1785	4,558	3,009	1,154	587	2,308	1,236	
	4,258	2,886	2,242	889	1,603	1,336	I
	4,185	3,060	1,551	728	2,014	1,733	45
	4,471	3,655	1,431	735	1,886	1,766	14
	5,241 4·2°	3,924 2·4°	1,957 1·3°	670 0·6°	2,525 1·6°	1,764 1·5°	28
1790	4,913	3,314	2,386	929	3,432	1,986	31 0·03°
	5,323	3,971	2,272	856	4,225	2,649	39
	6,084	4,228	2,438	1,368	4,271	2,922	56
	5,739	2,039	2,722	385	3,515	2,695	107
	9,649	2,126	2,922	750	3,860	3,633	21
1795	10,045	2,412	2,383	429	5,254	2,461	54
	8,317	2,457	2,377	614	6,054	3,223	206
	9,185	1,587	2,288	887	5,057	3,144	1,041
	10,139	1,405	1,146	1,291	5,580	5,198	665
	7,939 7·6°	2,099 2·6°	2,436 2·3°	1,622 0·9°	7,057 4·7°	5,947 3·3°	1,264
1800	14,325	3,404	2,860	1,099	7,866	4,087	1,048 0·4°
	14,442	3,545	2,946	1,124	7,518	4,386	479
	15,015	7,752	2,930	1,161	5,329	3,926	589
	11,372	3,968	2,733	819	5,273	2,380	285
	12,716	3,033	1,766	1,173	6,398	4,282	193
1805	13,026	2,440	1,669	991	7,147	3,832	312
	10,533	2,678	1,037	1,433	8,613	4,734	319
	9,412	3,278	1,884	798	7,921	4,579	1,796
	4,734	6,547	1,933	533	3,992	5,929	4,830
	13,666 12·9°	10,055 4·6°	1,648 2·1°	706 1·0°	5,188 6·5°	5,975 4·4°	6,382 1·5°
1810	11,221	8,385	1,717	484	7,813	4,790	5,970
	2,358	12,066	1,665	317	1,432	4,123	3,047
	5,460	15,528	1,779	444	4,136	4,767	4,115
1813	—	—	—	—	—	—	—
	22,922	12,348	1,698	422		6,315	4,302
1815	19,860	9,071	2,093	393	11,937	6,916	3,786
	18,493	9,000	2,205	380	7,800	4,608	3,284
	16,988	9,529	2,795	506	6,377	6,762	4,882
	17,181	10,141	3,196	479	8,383	5,785	5,552
	16,016 13·0°	9,441 9·5°	2,422 2·1°	423 0·4°	4,302 5·8°	4,490 5·4°	3,472 4·1°
1820	18,982	10,693	3,391	566	3,921	4,353	4,450
	16,052	11,264	4,428	684	6,607	5,069	4,927
	15,358	13,932	4,101	682	7,368	4,146	5,323

Tables 4 and 5 Notes

Tables 4 and 5 show the ultimate failure of the plantation empire to play a real role in the national economy of the nineteenth century.

Table 4 shows that up to 1820 the British West Indies were a major source of imports to Great Britain, equal to Europe and greater than any of the other regions listed. However this contribution was in part due to protection and preference.

By 1854 imports from Europe, U.S.A., South America, India and Asia had all surpassed those from the West Indies, which had not increased. Africa, Canada and Australia had caught up with the West Indies colonies.

After the removal of all preferences and protection in 1854, the West Indian colonies continued at about the same level of imports until the 1880s when the competition of much bigger and more efficient producers finally overwhelmed them. By the end of the century Africa and New Zealand had both passed the West Indian figure.

It should be noted that at the end of the century Europe was still producing about half the British imports and U.S.A. nearly a quarter.

Table 5 shows something of a similar pattern. At the end of the period Europe was taking about 45 per cent of British exports, while Asia was a more valuable customer than U.S.A. There are two massive unfavourable trade balances, with Europe sending £106 million more to us than they bought from us, and the U.S.A. £80 million, although it must be stressed that this is only the *trade* balance and not the total balance of payments. Africa ended the period as a highly promising market, and the Asian market expanded all through the century. In 1910 all the markets, including New Zealand, had surpassed the West Indies, which had shown very little movement as a market during the century.

These figures themselves explain the abandonment of the plantation colonies vividly. They were not big enough, efficient enough or wealthy enough to be taken into the reckoning of the workshop of the world.

Table 4 Imports in Ten-year Averages by Regions of Origin in millions

DATE	1780–89	1790–99	1800–09	1810–19	1854–59	1860–69	1870–79	1880–89	1890–99
N. Europe	3·8	5·3	5·8	4·9	60·6	96·4	147·5	165·2	192·1
S. Europe	1·8	2·4	2·7	3·2	(N.+S. Europe combined above)				
Asia	2·4	3·8	4·8	5·9	26·8	50·9	52·2	56·0	45·1
Africa	0·07	0·08	0·1	0·2	5·6	6·2	8·0	8·6	9·3
Canada	0·2	0·2	0·4	0·6	5·9	7·4	10·5	10·9	15·6
U.S.A.	0·5	1·2	2·0	2·2	31·9	34·9	70·9	90·7	104·5
B.W.I./Foreign W.I.	3·2	4·4	7·7	8·0	7·7	9·8	8·7	3·9	1·9
S. America	0·08	0·5	1·7	3·4	12·8	19·3	23·6	17·5	19·4
India (inclu. in Asia)	+	+	+	+	14·9	33·8	29·4	33·5	26·1
Australia					5·1	8·6	15·4	19·6	22·2
New Zealand					0·1	1·1	3·3	5·5	8·5

Table 5 British Exports by Regions, Shown as Ten-year Averages in millions

DATE	1820–29	1830–39	1840–49	1850–59	1860–69	1870–79	1880–89	1890–99	1900–09
N. Europe	8·5	10·2	14·0	31·7	56·8	86·9	77·9	86·1	119·0
S. Europe	6·6	7·7	10·6	(N.+S. Europe combined above)					
Africa	0·5	1·1	1·7	2·6	4·0	8·3	8·6	15·0	25·8
Asia	4·1	5·4	9·4	15·1	29·5	34·4	48·2	48·2	70·7
U.S.A.	5·7	7·9	6·7	17·2	20·2	25·7	28·1	22·1	24·2
B.W.I.	3·4	3·0	2·7	3·4	4·8	5·7	4·7	3·9	4·3
Central and S. America	4·2	4·8	5·4	9·3	15·5	18·9	21·3	22·8	30·0
India	3·6	3·6	5·4	10·6	18·7	21·8	30·6	29·4	36·2
Australia and S. Pacific	0·3+	0·7+	1·3+	8·2	10·4	13·1	19·1	16·7	20·4
Canada	1·5	2·1	2·8	4·3	4·9	7·9	8·2	6·5	12·2
New Zealand				0·3	1·6	3·1	3·5	6·8	

Bibliography

GENERAL

Two good general histories of the British West Indies are:

1 Parry, J. H. and Sherlock, P. M., *A Short History of the West Indies*, Macmillan 1956.

2 Burn, W. L., *The British West Indies*, Hutchinson University Library 1951.

3 Williams, Eric, *Capitalism and Slavery*, Deutsch 1964: a passionate and brilliant reinterpretation of the whole problem, rather overstated as the result of the author's multiple biases.

4 Fieldhouse, D. K., *The Colonial Empires*, Weidenfeld & Nicolson 1966: a recent and comprehensive analysis of an enormous subject.

5 and 6 *The Cambridge History of the British Empire*, vols. I and II: useful articles by a generation of great historians of empire, notably C. M. Andrews, Lilian Penson, Cecil Headlam, J. F. Rees, Vincent Harlow, Coupland, J. H. Clapham, A. P. Newton and H. J. Habbakuk.

7, 8, 9 and 10 *The New Cambridge Modern History*, vols. VII, VIII, IX, X: disappointing in its treatment of colonial affairs, but contains valuable chapters by Frank Thistlethwaite (7), J. H. Parry (7), Habbakuk (8), H. G. Schenk (9) and H. Heaton (10).

11 Deerr, N., *The History of Sugar*, Chapman and Hall 1949, 2 vols.

EARLY SOURCES

There is a fine collection of contemporary literature on the West Indies, but not easy to come by.

12 Edwards, Bryan, *The History of the British Colonies in the West Indies*, 1801–7: an excellent and sympathetic work by a West Indian supporter of slavery.

146

13 Lewis, M. G. ('Monk'), *The Journal of a West Indian Proprietor, 1816*: the work of a sympathetic absentee proprietor and author after a visit to his estates.

14 Newton, J., *The Journal of a Slave Trader, 1750–54*, ed. B. Martin and M. Spurrell. Epworth Press 1962: important as the author became a leading abolitionist.

15 Park, Mungo, *Travels in the interior of Africa*, 1799, Dent (Everyman): another important source, showing the ravages of the slave trade far inland.

16 Carlyle, Thomas, 'An occasional discourse on the nigger question', reprinted in *Essays*, Dent (Everyman), vol. 2: a revealing document.

ASPECTS OF TRADE

17 Ramsay, G., *English Trade in the Centuries of Emergence*, Macmillan, 1957: has useful chapters on the western ports and the Atlantic system.

18 Parkinson, C. N., ed., *The Trade Winds*, Allen & Unwin, 1948: a study of British Overseas Trade, 1793–1816, with a strong list of authors, including the editor, C. M. MacInnes, Lucy Horsfall and H. Heaton.

THE SLAVE TRADE AND AFRICA

19 Davies, K. G., *The Royal African Company*, Longmans 1957: a definitive account of the attempt to establish a monopoly in the trade, and very revealing about the attitude of the West Indians to the trade.

20 Lawrence, A. W., *Trade Castles and Forts of West Africa*, Cape 1963: full on its subject, and worth looking at for its marvellous photographs.

21 Lloyd, C., *The Navy and the Slave Trade*, Longmans 1949: covers the period after abolition interestingly.

22 Mannix, J. P. and Cowley, M., *Black Cargoes*, Longmans 1963: the best recent account of the trade.

23 Langdon-Davies, John, ed., *The Slave Trade and its Abolition*, Cape (Jackdaw series) 1965: worth seeing for its reproductions of contemporary illustrative material.

24 Davidson, Basil, *Black Mother*, Gollancz 1961.

25 Herskovits, M., *The Myth of the Negro Past*, Boston, Mass. 1964.

Nos 24 and 25 are valuable for the African background.

147

26 Davidson, B., ed., *The African Past*, Longmans 1964; Penguin 1966.

27 MacInnes, C. M., *Bristol and the Slave Trade*, Bristol Branch, Historical Association, 1963.

THE WEST INDIES

The late Professor Pares has produced a series of elegant and fruitful books on the Caribbean. These include:

28 Pares, R., *Yankees and Creoles*, Longmans 1956: on the trade between the American and Caribbean colonies.

29 Pares, R., *Merchants and Planters*, Cambridge U.P. 1960 (Economic History Review Supplement).

30 Pares, R., *A West Indian Fortune*, Longmans 1950: a great study of the Pinney family in Nevis and Bristol.

31 Pares, R., *War and Trade in the West Indies* 1739–63, Oxford U.P. 1936: a pioneer work of great detail.

32 Armytage, F., *The Free Port System in the West Indies*, Longmans 1953.

33 Patterson, Orlando, *The Sociology of Slavery*, MacGibbon and Kee 1967: examines the slave in the setting of the plantation.

For particular islands:

34 Williams, Eric, *A History of the People of Trinidad and Tobago*, Deutsch 1964: has some useful material, but was clearly assembled at breakneck speed for an occasion.

35 Harlow, V., *The History of Barbados*, Oxford U.P. 1926.

36 Curtin, P. D., *Two Jamaicas*, Cambridge U.P. 1955: analyses the conflict of ideas during and after emancipation.

37 Smith, M. G., *The Plural Society in the British West Indies*, University of California Press 1965: traces characteristics of modern Jamaica back to the slave period.

38 Metcalf, G., *Royal Government and Political Government in Jamaica, 1729–1823*, Longmans 1965.

39 Boxer, C. R., *The Dutch Seaborne Empire*, Hutchinson 1965: treats the whole Dutch colonial effort, but is thin on the Caribbean area.

40 Parry, J. H., *The Spanish Seaborne Empire*, Hutchinson 1966: in the same series as (**39**), reminds the reader of the vast size and resilience of the Spanish empire in the period. (**4**) is the best treatment of the French colonies in English, but L. Gershoy is preparing a volume in the Hutchinson series.

41 Leyburn, J., *The Haitian People*, New Haven, Yale U.P. 1941.
42 James, C. L. R., *The Black Jacobins*, Secker & Warburg 1938.

THE AMERICAN COLONIES

Since there is an enormous literature on this subject, this selection is very subjective.

43 Boorstin, D., *The Americans: the Colonial Experience*, Penguin 1965: a brilliant and convincing analysis of aspects of colonial life, and particularly valuable for Virginia and Georgia.
44 Christie, I., *Crisis of Empire*, Edward Arnold 1966.
45 Versteeg, C., *The Formative Years 1607–1763*, Macmillan 1965.
46 Gipson, L., *The Coming of the Revolution*, Hamilton 1954.
47 Mackesy, Piers, *The War for America 1775–1783*, Longmans 1964.
48 Stampp, K., *The Peculiar Institution*, Eyre & Spottiswoode 1964: deals with slavery after the revolution, but is valuable for contrast.

ENGLAND

The subject is so integral to English history in this period that only a few works can be singled out.

49 Wilson, C., *England's Apprenticeship*, Longmans 1965.
50 Ashton, T. S., *An Economic History of England: the 18th Century*, Oxford U.P. 1948.
51 Namier, L., *England in the Age of the American Revolution*, Macmillan 1930.
52 Harlow, V., *The Founding of the Second British Empire*, vol. 1, Longmans 1952: a close examination of the shift of interest from a plantation empire to a commercial empire.
53 Madden, A. F. McC., 'The Imperial Machinery of the Younger Pitt' in *Essays in British History*, Macmillan 1964: traces continuity in government policy after the American Revolution.
54 Carswell, J., *The South Sea Bubble*, Cresset Press 1960.
55 McLachlan, J. O., *Trade and Peace with Old Spain 1667–1750*, Cambridge U.P. 1940.

ABOLITION OF SLAVERY

There is also a massive literature on the emancipation struggle, much of it overwritten.

56 Coupland, R., *The British Anti-Slavery Movement*, Home University Library of Modern Knowledge 1933.

149

57 Warner, Oliver, *William Wilberforce*, Batsford 1962.

58 Burn, W. L., *Emancipation and Slavery in the British West Indies*, Cape 1937.

59 Fyfe, C., *A History of Sierra Leone*, Oxford U.P. 1962.

IDEAS AND THEORY

60 Bennett, G., ed., *The Concept of Empire*, A. and C. Black 1955.

61 Winch, D., *Classical Political Economy and Colonies*, L. S. E. Bell 1965.

62 Knorr, K., *British Colonial Theories, 1570–1850*, University of Toronto Press 1944.

63 Harlow, V. and Madden, A. F., *British Colonial Developments 1774–1834*, Oxford U.P. 1953.

64 Schumpeter, E., *English Overseas Trade Statistics 1697–1908*, Oxford U.P. 1960.

65 Mitchell, B. R. and Deane, P., *Abstract of British Historical Statistics*, Cambridge U.P. 1962.

66 Wilson, C., *Mercantilism*, Historical Association 1958.

ARTICLES

67 Penson, Lillian M., 'The London West Indian interest in the 18th century', *English Historical Review*, xxxvi, 1921; reprinted in *Essays in 18th-Century History from the E.H.R.*, ed. R. Mitchison, Longmans 1966.

68 Whitridge, Arnold, 'The American Slave Trade', *History Today*.

69 Hyde, F. E., Parkinson, B. B. and Marriner, S., 'The nature and profitability of the Liverpool slave trade', *Economic History Review*, 2nd ser., v, no. 3.

70 Pares, R., 'The London sugar market, 1740–69', *Economic History Review*, 2nd ser., ix, 1956.

71 Pares, R., 'The Economic factors in the history of empire', *Economic History Review*, 1st ser., vii, 1937; reprinted in *Essays in Economic History*, vol. 1, ed. E. M. Carus-Wilson, Edward Arnold 1954.

72 Pares, R., 'American versus continental warfare, 1739–63', *English Historical Review*, li, 1936; reprinted in *The Historian's Business*, Oxford U.P. 1961.

73 Davies, K. G., 'The origin of the commission system in West Indian trade', *Transactions of Royal Historical Society*, 5th ser., ii, 1952.

150

74 Phillips, U. B., 'A Jamaican slave plantation', *American Historical Review* xix (1913/14).

75 Farnie, D. A., 'The commercial empire of the Atlantic, 1607–1783', *Economic History Review*, 2nd ser., xv, 1963.

76 —— 'English foreign trade, 1700–74', *Economic History Review*, 2nd ser., xiv, 1962.

77 Robinson, R. and Gallagher, J., 'The imperialism of free trade', *Economic History Review*, 2nd ser., vi, 1953.

78 Macdonagh, O., 'The Anti-imperialism of free trade', *Economic History Review*, 2nd ser., xiv, 1962.

79 Williams, J. E., 'Whitehaven in the eighteenth Century', *Economic History Review*, 2nd ser., viii, no. 3, 1956.

Index

Index